Christian Eichler

SOCCER
365 Days

Foreword by Alexi Lalas

Translated from the German by Matthew D. Gaskins

Abrams, New York

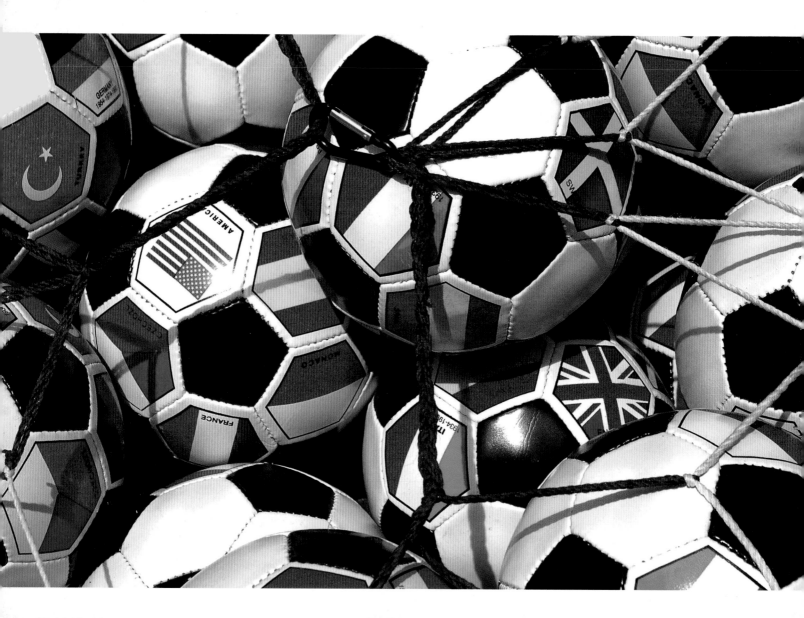

Foreword // By Alexi Lalas, member of 1994 USA World Cup team

Soccer is a strange and beautiful game. It's not for everybody, but there's something for everybody in it. It's not a sport that provides instant gratification; it usually makes you work for it. It can offer electrifying moments of brilliance followed by relative periods of calm. It unites and divides, elates and maddens. It's a puzzle that unravels in ninety minutes.

Soccer is the most popular sport in the world, period. It defies political, social, and economic boundaries, and is often the common thread linking cultures and nations. Every four years, the world comes together to celebrate this thread in an unrivaled spectacle that is the World Cup.

I grew up in suburban Detroit, just another kid playing youth soccer on the weekends. I had Mom and Dad coaching, orange peels and juice boxes at halftime, and I was about as far away from a World Cup as you can get. I had no idea that someday I would be fortunate enough to represent the United States in the esteemed international tournament.

But, as it has done to so many, soccer pulled me in and refused to let me go. The limited rules, the constant flow of play, and the lack of coaching interference meant that my actions had a remarkably influential impact in determining the outcome. Even after I had reached the top of my sport, I always loved the fact that there was never only one right answer in soccer. Each game, each minute, and each play is dictated by the players.

For a soccer player, participating in a World Cup is the ultimate achievement. No matter what successes you may have had at the club level, representing your country in a World Cup trumps it all. It's where stars are born and legends are cemented. Governments shut down, companies halt production, and countries become silent while their teams play. A country's pride is on the line and the world is watching.

Each World Cup produces moments that define it, on and off the field. The goals, the saves, and the results will go down in the record books, but the host country often will play a part in this history. The diversity of fans and their cultures create a unique celebration in the stadiums and in the cities. The passion, the color, and the party are vital elements of the world's biggest sporting event.

I lived the power of what a World Cup can do to an individual, and I saw the impact it can have on a country. In 1994, I was part of the USA World Cup team, and millions of people across America and billions of people around the world watched as we competed against the best. To this day, people remember the summer of 1994 and what it meant for soccer in the United States.

World Cups are memorable because of their grandeur and global relevance. So enjoy this historical look at the World Cups, the games, the players, the fans, the countries, and the stadiums. Ultimately, a World Cup is a celebration of the one thing we can all agree upon: Soccer is the greatest game in the world.

Introduction // A History of the World Cup

Soccer conquered the world overnight. First, it had to break away from its cousin, rugby, which up to this very day has not managed to spread much beyond the British Commonwealth. This separation occurred in 1863 with the founding of the English Football Association and the drafting of the Laws of the Game. In contrast to rugby, the Laws set strict limits on the use of the hands—for soccer, this meant players weren't allowed to use their hands to hold the ball or an opponent. This made the game difficult, but interesting. We all know that nature created the hand—not the foot—for everything that requires skill. After all, it's difficult to eat, write, use a screwdriver, or play the violin with your feet. But, in the end, soccer offered a sensible use for this highly undervalued part of the body. Someone should have thought of it earlier. When you consider it, gravity causes the ball to fall back to the ground sooner or later, where the next closest thing is the foot. Thus, from the very beginning, soccer was connected to the earth's gravity—and almost overnight, countless fans and players worldwide gravitated toward the new sport.

As good missionaries of fitness training, the English brought a few leather balls and the rules of this new, undemanding game with them wherever they happened to land in the late nineteenth century—from Burma to Brazil. Their influence fell on fruitful soil. It was as if the game were made for poor countries—to play, all you needed was a ball and a free space.

Yet it didn't take long for soccer to get organized. Around the world, clubs, associations, and leagues were formed. Sometimes, early fans played simple pickup games in the streets—barefoot and ball crazy. Other times, groups of workers got together, finding in soccer a cheap, new way to entertain themselves in their free time. And sometimes the players were privileged students and sons of the well-to-do. It was not uncommon in the Ruhr district of

Germany—the heartland of German soccer—for business owners, mostly publicans, to become involved, for they recognized new business opportunities in the sport. The restaurant proprietor Willi Heinig, for example, contributed to the creation of the FC Schalke 04 by investing money in the construction of a playing field. His plan worked; the players would play soccer first, and then afterward they went to his bar. When a Catholic youth group founded the other large club in the Ruhr area in 1909, it provoked a nasty fight between the players and their chaplain, who vehemently fought his pupils' new hobby—in the end, however, with little success.

While people fought with their own two hands for soccer's survival in some places, elsewhere its global fate was being planned already. As early as 1905, at the second meeting of the Fédération Internationale de Football Association (FIFA) in Paris, the Dutchman Carl Hirschmann suggested the creation of a world championship in soccer. People were excited by the idea; they arranged for a trophy, organized space for games in Switzerland, divided up the twelve participants—but, unfortunately, nobody ended up wanting to participate. At this point, they were a few decades ahead of the game.

In the late 1920s, soccer finally had become a worldwide phenomenon. Profes-

 < 1958 Sweden

 < 1962 Chile

 < 1966 England

sional leagues were formed all over Europe following the English model, whose players had been paid since 1888 for their kicking efforts. Tens of thousands of viewers flooded the stadiums and celebrated their heroes. After the collapse of old dynasties and social structures in World War I, two new mass phenomena took over the reins: cinema and sports. Whereas millions of people used to pay tribute to emperors and kings, they now had a ravenous appetite for news about their new idols: movie stars and soccer heroes.

One of these new stars was José Luis Andrade, who won the Olympic gold medal with Uruguay's team in 1924 and thrilled the Parisian public with his light-footed style, which, until that point, had never been seen in Europe. Back then, however, FIFA was suspicious of the fact that the

Olympic soccer tournament had become a sort of stand-in world championship.

The World Cup's premiere thus took place in Uruguay in 1930. Yet the event that today stirs the hearts of billions of people across the globe sparked so little interest at the time that it was nearly canceled. Two months before the tournament, no single European country had voiced its commitment. The British were not in FIFA, and the Germans insisted on their amateur rules prohibiting all contact with professionals; others turned down the invitation because of the long trip, the Great Depression, and the problem of borrowing the players from their employers for months on end. Because of all this, the infuriated South Americans even threatened to pull out of the international association.

An alarmed Jules Rimet, then FIFA president, was at least successful in securing the

1970 >
Mexico

1974 >
Germany

1978 >
Argentina

participation of his homeland, France, by ensuring that the Peugeot factories in Sochaux gave the players time off. He also negotiated with the army, which employed two of France's players. Belgium and Yugoslavia then signed up, and in Romania it proved to be a lucky twist of fate that King Carol II was the general secretary of the soccer association: he simply issued a royal order that his country participate. After the Europeans arrived in Montevideo, following strenuous train trips and a fifteen-day passage on the Conte Verde, which included occasional training on deck, the world championship could go on, thus marking the birth of the most popular sporting event in the world.

It was a debut full of odd happenings. The first goal in world championship history was scored in sleet (it was winter in the southern hemisphere), and was celebrated by the Frenchmen Lucien Laurent and his teammates in a French brothel in Montevideo, complete with Alsatian sauerkraut. Hector Castro, a one-armed forward, shot the last goal of the tournament for a 4–2 final victory for Uruguay over Argentina. The events that fell between the first and the last goal included a game that the referee called after only eighty-four minutes (instead of ninety); a penalty kick that was shot from at least fifteen yards (as opposed to the standard twelve yards—someone had forgotten to chalk the penalty spot); and the U.S. team's manager at one point running onto the field, protesting all the while, and dropping his bag—thus breaking a bottle of chloroform that he had in it, which caused him to fall unconscious. There were games with as few as

< 1982
Spain

< 1986
Mexico

< 1990
Italy

three hundred spectators, but there were also games with so many spectators that entire countries ended up paralyzed by mass euphoria. A total of ninety thousand fans watched the final game, for example, and public life in Montevideo came to a complete standstill on both sides of the Río de la Plata.

The coverage in the European press was spotty, at best. The sports journals had to wait for their special correspondent, the Belgian John Langenus, to make the long trip back. Consequently, the first detailed report on the world championship appeared only weeks later. At this point, the world championship still stood in the margins of public interest. This changed quickly. In Italy in 1934, when the home team won the title as the dictator Benito Mussolini had ordered, and when it later successfully defended the title in France in 1938, the World Cup became an event in Europe as well—before its development was put on hold for twelve years due to World War II. Even the postwar premiere in Brazil in 1950 was not a full-fledged world championship. Many countries were still suffering from the aftermath of the war, and without the sixteen teams needed for a true World Cup, the field was not really complete.

Yet with the World Cup in 1954, the stage was set for the sport's success story. It was a tournament of splendid offensive style, legendary teams, and a sensational final— all broadcast on television for the first time ever. Soccer's image had taken flight, and has remained aloft ever since. Over the past

1994 >
U.S.

1998 >
France

2002 >
South Korea & Japan

fifty years, the World Cup has become an event that attracts millions of fans, makes billions of dollars for the television industry, and supports entire national economies. Indeed, the championship is one of the largest myth-making machines in the history of mankind, and it feeds the hunger of a public looking for new role models and grand heroes.

Part of the World Cup's success has to do with the fact that it has not been over-hyped like many other sporting events. In our modern times of interchangeable sit-coms, light entertainment, and talk shows concerned only with the hot topics of the day, the four years between each championship leave space and time for memories to sink in. For many, each World Cup becomes a small piece of their own private histories. At the same time, it is an event that creates memories that unite entire nations.

Rahn, the rain, and the Miracle of Bern in 1954. Pelé's breathtaking debut in 1958. Garrincha's dribbling skills in 1962. The Wembley goal of 1966. The Game of the Century in 1970. Cruyff & Co.'s Total Soccer in 1974. Cordoba's humiliation in 1978. Brazil's beautiful failure in 1982. Demigod Maradona in 1986. Germany's joy after reunification in 1990. Italy's penalty kick drama in 1994. The second French Revolution in 1998. Ronaldo's spectacular show in 2002. Every tournament has left behind powerful memories. And the only prediction we can make with confidence in soccer: the World Cup in 2006 will do so as well.

Germany's World Cup victory of 1954 came to be known as the Miracle of Bern. The fact that a film of the same name became one of the largest successes in German cinema half a century later shows just how much the myth of Bern continues to speak to the German people. Indeed, the victory over the Hungarian Wonder Team offered them a kind of emotional liberation; it was a story full of dramatic elements broadcast in electrifying radio reports. Later, scholars even went as far as to claim that the victory anticipated the Federal Republic of Germany becoming a sovereign nation. Without a doubt, it was difficult after the war for many neighboring countries to bear the sight of the triumphant Germans—not least when thousands of spectators in the stadium had struck up the verse "*Deutschland über alles*" (Ger-

many above all), which had only recently been stricken from the German national anthem for its nationalist tenor. In the end, however, Bern did not end up having negative political consequences. The young republic had become too much a part of the new Europe for old fears to be revived by a soccer game, particularly since the humble soccer of the German team didn't come anywhere close to fulfilling the cliché of martial, goose-stepping Germans. On the soccer front, it was a spectacular World Cup, full of offensive plays and lots of goals. For the best soccer team, however, it was a tragedy. Hungary's Wonder Team hadn't lost a single game in five years—but it was this, of all games, that put an end to their winning streak. This was a team that had revolutionized soccer, and yet their reward was to be denied a second chance: after the quashed rebellion against Soviet rule in 1956, the team was scattered to the four winds.

// The Games

FIRST ROUND, GROUP A

Brazil vs. Mexico 5–0
Yugoslavia vs. France 1–0
France vs. Mexico 3–2
Brazil vs. Yugoslavia 1–1 OT

RESULTS
1. Yugoslavia (Points: 3, Goals: 2–1;
won tiebreaker for top seeding)
2. Brazil (3, 6–1)
3. France (2, 3–3)
4. Mexico (0, 2–8)

FIRST ROUND, GROUP C

Uruguay vs. Czechoslovakia 2–0
Austria vs. Scotland 1–0
Uruguay vs. Scotland 7–0
Austria vs. Czechoslovakia 5–0

RESULTS
1. Austria (Points: 4, Goals: 6–0;
won tiebreaker for top seeding)
2. Uruguay (4, 9–0)
3. Czechoslovakia (0, 0–7)
4. Scotland (0, 0–8)

FIRST ROUND, GROUP B

Germany vs. Turkey 4–1
Hungary vs. South Korea 9–0
Hungary vs. Germany 8–3
Turkey vs. South Korea 7–0
Germany vs. Turkey 7–2 (playoff)

RESULTS
1. Hungary (Points: 4, Goals: 17–3)
2. Germany (2, 14–11)
3. Turkey (2, 10–11)
4. South Korea (0, 0–16)

FIRST ROUND, GROUP D

England vs. Belgium 4–4 OT
Switzerland vs. Italy 2–1
Italy vs. Belgium 4–1
England vs. Switzerland 2–0
Switzerland vs. Italy 4–1 (playoff)

RESULTS
1. England (Points: 3, Goals: 6–4)
2. Switzerland (2, 6–4)
3. Italy (2, 6–7)
4. Belgium (1, 5–8)

OT = Overtime
PEN = Penalty-kick shoot-out

QUARTERFINALS

Austria vs. Switzerland 7–5
Uruguay vs. England 4–2
Hungary vs. Brazil 4–2
Germany vs. Yugoslavia 2–0

SEMIFINALS

Germany vs. Austria 6–1
Hungary vs. Uruguay 4–2 OT

THIRD-PLACE MATCH

Austria vs. Uruguay 3–1

FINAL

Germany vs. Hungary 3–2

World Cup Champion: GERMANY

Of course in order to play soccer, you need both feet. But being able to play the ball equally well with either foot is a skill that takes years to develop and requires hours upon hours of shooting practice. The ability to kick the ball just as cleanly with the left and right foot—and with enough power to pose a serious goal-scoring threat—is what distinguishes the accomplished player from all the rest. One of the best strikers of all time was Tom Finney, the counterpart to legendary Stanley Matthews. He participated in seventy-six national games for England. In itself, this may not be unusual, but his brilliant ability to play both sides certainly was: he played forty-three games as a right wing and thirty-three as a left wing.

4 // January

> Jock Aird (left) has as much of a chance man-on-man with Julio César Abbadie as the whole Scottish team against the superior Uruguayans.

....

....

....

....

Generally speaking, a World Cup team consists of twenty-two players. But why take eleven extras with you, when only eleven can play? At least this is what coach Andy Beattie thought, thus confirming the stereotype of Scottish frugality. Unfortunately, the Scots were also sparing with goals. They lost with an embarrassing 0–7 defeat to Uruguay following a 0–1 loss to Austria. ⚽

5 // January

> Goalkeeper Seren Turgay attacks the German striker Hans Schäfer, yet can't prevent the equalizer, which brings the score to 1–1. Germany wins the first game against Turkey 4–1.
< The German striker Ottmar Walter (left) and the Turkish midfielder Izak Rober.

The procedure governing the World Cup tournament has always combined to varying degrees the basic round-robin principles of division sports (where each team plays against every other team, mostly in the qualifying rounds) and the single-elimination tournament system (the winner progresses, the loser is eliminated, mostly in the preliminary round or the quarterfinals). Yet at no other tournament was such a grossly unfair system used as in 1954. The four teams in the qualifying rounds were divided into high-seeded and low-seeded teams that were then pitted against each other, so the games weren't equally matched. In the end, this meant that a low-seeded team had to beat a high-seeded team twice in order to proceed to the next round. Germany, for example, beat Turkey 4–1 in the group game and then again in the deciding match, 7–2. Host Switzerland had to beat Italy twice to reach the quarterfinals.

> > Ertan Mustafa (left) gets past the German goalkeeper Toni Turek; Karl Mai can do little more than watch. In the end Germany beats Turkey for the second time, 7–2.
> < The German midfielder Horst Eckel (middle) shoots the ball past the Turkish goalkeeper Ersoy Sükrü, tucking it neatly into the net.

Germany's coach, Sepp Herberger, was at first reviled for what turned out to be a smart decision. Only later was he praised for it. He took numerous regular players out of the group game against the favorites, Hungary, to save them for the decisive match against Turkey. Germany proceeded to suffer an embarrassing 3–8 loss to Hungary's Wonder Team. But Herberger didn't let this upset him. With their batteries recharged, his team was able to sail to victory in their second game against Turkey. When Germany and Hungary encountered each other in the final, the Hungarian players ended up clearly underestimating their opponents, in part due to their memory of their earlier 8–3 victory. Almost immediately afterward, everyone was raving about Herberger's "bluff," even though he actually only had been trying to budget his team's strength. In the end, Herberger earned himself a reputation as the sharp fox of coaching. ⚽

7 // January

June 26, 1954, went down as one of the hottest and craziest days in World Cup history. Two quarterfinal games took place in the stifling heat, and a total of eighteen goals were scored. While world champion Uruguay beat England 4–2 in Basel, the most goal-studded heat wave in soccer history took its toll in Lausanne. In this game, Austria won in temperatures over 95 degrees, and the 7–5 result is just as unprecedented as the sequence of goals: 0–3 (16th–18th minutes), 3–3 (25th–27th minutes), 5–3 (32nd–34th minutes), 5–4 (36th minute), 6–4 (54th minute), 6–5 (60th minute), 7–5 (77th minute). Austria's goalkeeper Kurt Schmied and Swiss captain Roger Bocquet suffered heat stroke. In fact, Schmied was so disoriented that he thought the game was over at half-time. Because substitutions weren't allowed, he had to play on. In the second half, the trainer stood behind the goal and told the barely conscious goalkeeper which way to jump. ⚽

8 // January

> Germany's captain, Fritz Walter (No. 16), is delighted with the 1–0 win over Yugoslavia—Ivan Horvat (on the ground), has just shot an own goal.

< The German team before the quarterfinal game against Yugoslavia.

....

....

....

....

An own goal: even the greatest soccer heroes are not immune to this form of humiliation. In the 1970s, Franz Beckenbauer scored twice against his own team in the national league—two games in a row, in fact. Before the start of the next game, his goalkeeper, Sepp Maier, couldn't help but ask, "So who's marking Beckenbauer on Saturday?" Beckenbauer wasn't really able to laugh about it. But of course it's nice your teammates don't lose their sense of humor when goals land in the wrong net—like Pentti Kekkola's teammates in the Finnish league. After his own goal tally reached five in the 1986 season, the team gave him a compass as a present. ⚽

1954 // Switzerland

9 // January

> Sándor Kocsis (No. 8) and Antenor Brandãozinho
(No. 4) fight over airspace in the quarterfinal
game Hungary vs. Brazil (4–2).
< The Brazilian Nilton Santos (left) and the
Hungarian captain József Bozsik after being
ordered off the field following a brawl.

People who witnessed the quarterfinal game between Hungary and Brazil christened it the Battle of Bern—perhaps the most brutal game in the history of the World Cup. "They behaved like people in an insane asylum," wrote the Zurich publication *Sport*. Three players were ordered off the field, there was a fight in the locker room and numerous injuries, and the local police had to intervene numerous times to maintain public order. Later, Brazil drafted a letter in protest against the English referee, who allegedly had acted "against Western Christian civilization in the service of international communism." ⚽

10 // January

> The Saint Jakob Stadium in Basel, venue of the semifinal game Germany vs. Austria, seated over fifty thousand spectators.

< The German striker Ottmar Walter (left) and the Austrian goalkeeper Walter Zeman.

With its innovative design—one side of the stadium had steep seating with an overhang, the other had deep rows of seats with a very low incline and no covering—the Saint Jakob Stadium in Basel is a prime example of early 1950s stadium architecture. Built specially for the World Cup, its open back and the train lines running behind provided a unique commercial opportunity. Train cars would stop behind the stadium, and passengers could watch the game from there for the mere sum of nine francs. ⚽

1954 // Switzerland

11 // January

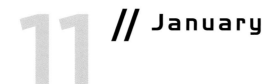

Germany vs. Austria: a special rivalry. Yet the score was never as one-sided as in the semifinal game of 1954. With the 6–1 victory for Germany, the outstanding Fritz Walter, who was involved in all six goals, succeeded along with his teammates in playing the best game that a German national team had ever played, according to eyewitnesses. While the Viennese poet Friedrich Torberg lamented the "most devastating defeat since Königgrätz," the German newspaper *Welt* triumphantly declared: "Alongside all the skill of the German team stood a wild resolve; the Austrians maintained a casual playfulness entirely devoid of strength. 'We are going to win,' said the Austrians, smiling before kickoff. 'We want to win,' said the Germans with grim determination. Two totally different worlds. It's no surprise that the men of the blue Danube lost the game." ⚽

1954 // Switzerland

12 // January

No other team has ever brought together two players who posed such a goal-scoring threat: Ferenc Puskás and Sándor Kocsis, who together scored over 150 goals for Hungary. Puskás had been badly injured in the qualifying round in 1954 by the German Werner Liebrich—thus leaving Kocsis to lead Hungary's Wonder Team into the finals all alone—with eleven goals in four games, including two headed goals for a 4–2 finish in overtime of the semifinal against Uruguay. Both men fled to the West in 1956 after the Hungarian Uprising was violently quashed by the Soviets. Puskás went on to enjoy a glorious late career with Real Madrid. Kocsis, "the Golden Head," however, had less luck with FC Barcelona. Homesick and plagued by business and health problems—his foot had to be amputated due to vascular disease—he took his own life at the age of forty-nine. ⚽

13 // January

> The Uruguayan goalkeeper Roque Gastón Máspoli throws himself at a ball shot by Austria's striker Erich Probst (left) in the game for third place, which Austria won 3–1.

< Karl Koller (above left) and Julio César Abbdadie (above right) caught in a header duel in the game for third place.

If goals are the spice of soccer life, then the 1954 World Cup offered a delicious spread: 140 goals in twenty-six games, an average of 5.38 per match, including the twelve-goal game between Austria and Switzerland. All in all, these are records that will probably never be matched. The 4-2-4 system (four defenders, two midfielders, four forwards) was developed by the little country of Paraguay, which succeeded in bringing this formation all the way up to first place in the South American championship—although one shouldn't forget that the tactic had been anticipated by the Hungarian Wonder Team. This offensive formation supplanted the more cautious system of the pre-war period. The *Rheinische Post* summed up the 1954 World Cup as "the rejection of an abortive development in soccer, with its excessive stress on force, speed, and destruction." ⚽

14 // January

Traditionally, soccer stadiums are functional buildings, usually located in the natural charm of industrial parks. Yet sometimes they are granted a permanent spot in the proverbial hall of soccer fame. Bern-Wankdorf became just such a place in German memory and remains so to this very day, even after being torn down in 2001. ⚽

15 // January

The year 1954 witnessed the only World Cup final ever played in the pouring rain. It was seen by the Germans as a sign of good luck. This had to do with the fact that their captain, Fritz Walter, could not bear the heat because it reminded him of a bout of malaria he suffered in Sicily during the war. Since Hungary's technical superiority was useless on the swampy pitch, this also meant that the Germans were rewarded for their stamina. It should be noted, too, that, in contrast to the Hungarians, the Germans had access to shoes with removable cleats, which had been developed by the equipment manager Adolf Dassler. The shoes used by the German team only weighed about 13 ounces, 8 ounces less than their steel-toed ancestors fifty years earlier. But it was still a long way to the light-footed 6-ounce shoes of today.

> Zoltan Czibor (middle) puts one past Germany's goalkeeper Toni Turek after eluding defender Werner Kohlmeyer (No. 3), bringing the score up to 2–0 for Hungary. The World Cup goal king Sandor Kocsis (No. 8) can do little more than watch.

< Germany's captain Fritz Walter.

If there was a turning point in soccer, then it was on November 25, 1953, when the dominance of the sport's inventors came to an end in London and soccer was reinvented. Hungary beat England 6–3 with a demonstration of modern soccer playing. What used to be a static contest based on positions was thus turned into a dynamic game spread over the entire pitch. Coach Gusztáv Sebes called this new style a crowning example of the ingenuity of the collective: Socialist Soccer. But the world was left to ask why this dream died. How could Hungary become the best team never to win the title? The answer: Standing eagle-eyed on that fateful day in the London stadium, Sepp Herberger figured out the Hungarians' weakness. On their right side, József Bozsik kept opening up holes in their field coverage by pushing forward as a sort of sixth striker. And what do you know? In the final game of 1954, all of the German goals were crossed from this side. ⚽

17 // January

> Hungary's goalkeeper Gyula Grosics on the ground, the ball in the goal: Helmut Rahn shoots in the 85th minute, scores, and secures a 3–2 win for Germany.

< The German team in a joyous outburst after winning the World Cup.

The best goals are actually pronounced "Gooooaaal!" The German goal with the most O's was scored by Helmut Rahn in 1954. Actually, it had to be that long, because most fans could only hear the game, not see it. In Germany, only about 27,952 people had television sets at the time. Thus, it's no wonder that the word "Goal!"—repeated three times by reporter Herbert Zimmermann—became the infant cry of the young Federal Republic. Around fifty million Germans heard it on the radio. But the triumphant progress of a new medium had already begun: This was the first World Cup to be shown on television. In Switzerland, you could even rent a television. It would turn on when you put a one-franc coin in, and once the retail price had been reached, it was considered paid-for. (Prices started at 995 francs.) The popularity of the World Cup made such a business practice unnecessary in Germany. The sale of televisions exploded on its own: in 1955, there were 170,000 TV sets, 1,000,000 in 1958, and in 1963 over 7,000,000. ⚽

> > A car in Germany's train, which the world champions used as a venue to celebrate on their way home.
>
> < The world champions' reception in the Munich Löwenbräu brewery: national coach Sepp Herberger, the proprietress, Fritz Walter, and Horst Eckel (from left).

Fearing reprisals from their fellow countrymen and the Stalinist governor Mátyás Rákosi, the Hungarian team was forced to switch to a secret platform when it arrived back in Budapest. The trip home for the German team, however, was a triumphant procession. The attention paid to the team by the adoring German public proved that the soccer miracle had merged with the economic miracle of postwar West Germany. Sausage packets, bouillon cubes, rain coats, name-brand underwear, cabinet televisions, motor scooters, "a half liter of good drinking milk, every day" for half a year, for each man twenty-four cans of beer a month, vacuum cleaners for married couples, coffee grinders for bachelors: the list of gifts reads like a department store catalog right out of the heyday of West German economic growth. The most far-sighted gift came by telegram from a hospital in Regensburg: "Free delivery (first class) for the first child born to a member of the German soccer team." ⚽

1958 // SWEDEN

Sweden witnessed an odd World Cup in 1958. It had perhaps the most exciting winning team in history, the most magnificent debut, the best dribbler, the most precise scorer—and the weakest audience. Even the home team's games weren't sold out. At the same time, the atmosphere at the Swedish games had been so artificially stoked up that the distressed opponents complained about a lack of fairness. For instance, the nature of the German defeat in the semifinal game awoke anti-Swedish sentiment in many back home. But all this quickly gave way to tolerance, as almost always happens when the usual surge of World Cup nationalism gradually subsides. What did last, however, was an enthusiasm for the football wizardry of the team with the

eye-catching sunshine yellow jerseys and green collars: none other than Brazil. Due to the similarity with their opponent Sweden's colors in the final game, Brazil's players had to give up their yellow and green in favor of blue jerseys with white shorts. But they won the title by a large margin nonetheless, and their performance was more inspiring than any other team before, or perhaps any team after. And no other player executed such a spectacular debut as the seventeen-year-old Pelé. He scored the winning goal in the quarterfinal game, a hat trick in the semifinal, and two goals in the final game. One of these goals remains a work of art: he lifted the ball out of the air, first propelling it over one Swedish player, then over another, and finally driving it into the net. In South America, a player who eludes his opponent in this way is said to be "wearing the ball like a hat." But for Pelé, it wasn't a hat—it was a crown.

SUÈDE · SWEDEN · SUECIA · SCHWEDEN 8 - 29. 6. 1958

FOOTBALL
FUTBOL
FUSSBALL

// The Games

FIRST ROUND, GROUP A

Germany vs. Argentina 3–1
Northern Ireland vs. Czechoslovakia 1–0
Germany vs. Czechoslovakia 2–2
Argentina vs. Northern Ireland 3–1
Germany vs. Northern Ireland 2–2
Czechoslovakia vs. Argentina 6–1
Northern Ireland vs. Czechoslovakia 2–1 OT (playoff)

RESULTS
1. Germany (Points: 4, Goals: 7–5)
2. Northern Ireland (3, 6–6)
3. Czechoslovakia (3, 9–6)
4. Argentina (2, 5–10)

FIRST ROUND, GROUP C

Sweden vs. Mexico 3–0
Wales vs. Hungary 1–1
Wales vs. Mexico 1–1
Sweden vs. Hungary 2–1
Sweden vs. Wales 0–0
Hungary vs. Mexico 4–0
Wales vs. Hungary 2–1 (playoff)

RESULTS
1. Sweden (Points: 5, Goals: 5–1)
2. Wales (3, 4–3)
3. Hungary (3, 7–5)
4. Mexico (1, 1–8)

FIRST ROUND, GROUP B

France vs. Paraguay 7–3
Yugoslavia vs. Scotland 1–1
Yugoslavia vs. France 3–2
Paraguay vs. Scotland 3–2
France vs. Scotland 2–1
Yugoslavia vs. Paraguay 3–3

RESULTS
1. France (Points: 4, Goals: 11–7)
2. Yugoslavia (4, 7–6)
3. Paraguay (3, 9–12)
4. Scotland (1, 4–6)

FIRST ROUND, GROUP D

Brazil vs. Austria 3–0
Soviet Union vs. England 2–2
Brazil vs. England 0–0
Soviet Union vs. Austria 2–0
England vs. Austria 2–2
Brazil vs. Soviet Union 2–0
Soviet Union vs. England 1–0 (playoff)

RESULTS
1. Brazil (Points: 5, Goals: 5–0)
2. Soviet Union (5, 5–4)
3. England (3, 4–5)
4. Austria (2, 2–7)

QUARTERFINALS

Germany vs. Yugoslavia 1–0
Brazil vs. Wales 1–0
Sweden vs. Soviet Union 2–0
France vs. Northern Ireland 4–0

SEMIFINALS

Sweden vs. Germany 3–1
Brazil vs. France 5–2

THIRD-PLACE MATCH

France vs. Germany 6–3

FINAL

Brazil vs. Sweden 5–2

World Cup Champion: BRAZIL

21 // January

> Agne Simonsson (middle) shoots the ball past Mexico's goalkeeper Antonio Carbajal for a 3–0 final score for Sweden.

1958 // Sweden

Antonio Carbajal was the first player to participate in five World Cups, not missing a single one from 1950–1966. But the Mexican goalkeeper and his team would experience almost nothing but losing, as they did in the opening game of 1958 against the host team, Sweden. Carbajal had his work cut out for him in this match and conceded numerous goals. In fact, he enjoyed only a single victory with his team—1962, in the last group match against Czechoslovakia, even though it was clear before the game that Mexico already had been eliminated. Because he had tried so many times, and yet the world championship trophy remained so far away, the organizers of the 1970 World Cup bestowed a special honor on the Mexican goalie in his homeland: at the final draw, he was allowed to present the trophy and have his photograph taken with it. ⚽

22 // January

> Scotland's goalkeeper Tommy Younger is beat—all clear for the Yugoslavian Aleksandar Petakovic, who notches a goal and brings the score to 1–0. The qualifier ended in a 1–1 draw.

For over a hundred years, technology ignored goalies. They played in cotton jerseys and wool pants, so-called Siberian Ovens that became completely waterlogged when it rained. And they would throw themselves at the ball—only to grab it with bare hands that by the end of the game would throb with pain. It was not until the 1960s that the first goalie gloves came on the market; they boasted rubber grips that originally had been used for ping-pong paddles. ⚽

23 // January

> The Soviet goalkeeper Lev Yashin secures the ball from the Englishman Derek Kevan.
< Nikita Simonian (Soviet Union) scores for a 1–0 lead in the England vs. Soviet Union qualifier (2–2).

The fact that England lost in the qualifying round—after a 2–2 draw, the team had to play yet again against the Soviet Union, losing this decisive game 0–1—was due to a great tragedy: the Busby Babes' plane crash. Busby Babes was the nickname for Manchester United, the English champion team coached by the legendary Scot Matt Busby, who had set out to challenge Real Madrid for the European Championship. Manchester United had reached the semifinals of the European Championship in Belgrade. But on the return trip, the team's airplane, after landing for a stopover, crashed in driving snow near Munich-Riem. Eight of the Busby Babes died, including the powerhouse core of the national team: Tommy Taylor, Roger Byrne, and Duncan Edwards, who was considered the talent of the century in English soccer. ⚽

24 // January

In the Soviet Union, there were high hopes of winning the title in the team's first World Cup. In addition to the outstanding goalkeeper Lev Yashin, the team boasted a young player who would later be called the "Russian Pelé": Eduard Streltsov. For many Russians, he was the biggest talent their country had ever produced. Yet the twenty-year-old was soon cut from the World Cup roster because he had refused the command to leave Torpedo Moscow to play for the army ZSKA club or the KGB Dynamo club. Perhaps his liaison with the daughter of a politburo member was his undoing. Whatever the reason, Eduard Streltsov disappeared for seven years to a work camp. He died at the age of fifty-two. In Russia, the heel pass is named after him. ⚽

25 // January

Colors have an intense symbolic power in soccer—they stand for belonging, team strength, tradition, and identity. The blue of the Italian jerseys, the golden yellow of Brazil, Germany's white, and the orange of Holland are signals of strength that impress the opponent and fire up a player's faith in himself. The same goes, too, for the blue and white uniforms of Argentina's team. Yet this World Cup favorite played in unexpected attire in 1958. The striped jerseys of the Argentineans were too similar to the white German jerseys, at least according to referee Reginald Leafe. As a result, the South Americans had to play in shirts loaned from the local club Malmö FF—in yellow. No surprise that they lost 1–3. ⚽

1958 // Sweden

26 // January

Fans in South America are especially unforgiving of goalkeepers. While no one would think of holding a forward responsible for a failed attempt at a goal, a defeat that can be attributed to a goalkeeper can become a lifelong stigma. After the Brazilian Moacyr Barbosa suffered such a fate in 1950, the Argentinean Amadeo Carrizo—founder of the especially attack-oriented, complicated goalkeeping style in South American soccer (with successors like Gatti, Higuita, and Chilavert)—had to go through this as well. South American champion Argentina came to Sweden as a World Cup favorite but failed miserably. Yet Carrizo was the only player to be branded as an outcast in his country after the 1–6 loss to Czechoslovakia.

27 // January

> Uwe Seeler of Germany (right) isn't ready to give up the ball for lost, even though it's already in Czechoslovakian goalkeeper Bretislav Dolejsi's possession.

< Knees up: the Czechoslovak national team trains in the snow for the 1958 World Cup.

Fritz Walter, whom coach Sepp Herberger managed to talk into returning to the German national team in 1958 at the age of thirty-eight, and Uwe Seeler, World Cup rookie at the age of twenty-one, are not the most successful nor the most famous German players worldwide—but in Germany they are special favorites. They not only remained in Germany for their entire lives, but also stayed true to their home clubs. Walter stayed with Kaiserlautern, Seeler with Hamburg. Strong ties to one's roots tend to lead to enduring popularity, and this not only in Germany: the Dutchman Abe Lenstra, the "Uwe Seeler of Frisia," turned down every offer he got from foreign teams. As a result, hardly anyone knows him outside of Holland—but at home he is revered. In fact, one reader survey ranked Lenstra as one of the best Dutch players of all time, second only to Johan Cruyff and Marco van Basten. ⚽

1958 // Sweden

28 // January

> 1–0 Czechoslovakia: Milan Dvorak scores a penalty kick against the German goalie Fritz Herkenrath. The match ends 2–2.
< The Czechoslovakian team before leaving for Sweden.

When the penalty kick was adopted in the Laws of the Game—the official rules governing play—the gentleman footballers of soccer's dawning hours regarded it as an offense against the sport's honor: "A standing insult to sportsmen to have to play under a rule which assumes that players intend to trip, hack, and push opponents and to behave like cads of the most unscrupulous kidney," commented C. B. Fry, one of the best-known players of his time. Anger about the change has since subsided.

1958 // Sweden

> Sandor Matrai clears the ball here with a bicycle kick, but in the end Hungary finishes behind host Sweden 1–2.

< Brazil's legendary trainer Americo carries an injured Mazola off the pitch.

Today most people think that soccer has always had a real pull for spectators. But despite such unbelievable head counts like the two hundred thousand spectators in the Maracana Stadium in Rio for the decisive 1950 World Cup game between Brazil and Uruguay, it would be a mistake to assume that the game has always moved the masses as it does today. At the 1958 World Cup in Sweden, only one of the thirty-five games was sold out: the match between Brazil and Austria—and perhaps only because the stadium in Uddevalla held a mere 21,000 spectators. The home team's first four games filled only two-thirds of the stadium in Stockholm. Not even the semifinal against Germany and the final game against Brazil were sold out. ⚽

1958 // Sweden

30 // January

Double debut: Brazil played 0–0 against England, the first 0–0 draw in World Cup history. There was a small revolt within the team, and two new players joined the lineup: seventeen-year-old Pelé and twenty-four-year-old Garrincha. The Soviets had no clue what was happening to them; they couldn't guess that they were witnessing the World Cup debut of the best goal scorer and the greatest dribbler of all time. It was the beginning of a wonderful partnership: Brazil didn't lose a single game in which Pelé and Garrincha played together. ⚽

1958 // Sweden

31 // January

1958 // Sweden

"Thou shalt rest on the seventh day." Because of this biblical soccer rule, Northern Ireland's show at the World Cup hung for a moment in the balance. Representatives of the country's Protestant church had insisted that their prohibition against Sunday matches also be observed during the World Cup. In the end, though, an exception was granted, and the team was allowed to play. They beat the Soviet Union, played a 2–2 draw against Germany, and, above all, thanks to their fantastic goalie Harry Gregg, achieved the best result in their World Cup history: qualifying for the quarterfinals. ⚽

1 // February

> Laszlo Budai (Hungary, left) and John Charles in the decisive first-round game, in which Hungary loses to Wales 1–2.

Starting on May 14, 1950, with a 3–5 win over Austria, Hungary remained undefeated for thirty-one games—an incredible series of twenty-seven wins and four draws that ended in the 1954 World Cup final against Germany, of all opponents. Even to this day, this record remains unmatched by any other European team. Out of fifty games between 1950 and 1955, thirty-four of them were away games, and still Hungary won forty-two, played seven draws and lost only one game—the decisive one. Their goal differential: 215:58. After the bloody defeat of the Hungarian uprising against Soviet rule in 1956, the team fell apart and many players fled the country. In 1958, an aged Gyula Grosics, József Bozsik, and Nandor Hidegkuti were the only ones left, and all that remained of the Wonder Team was a pale reflection of its former self—certainly nothing that would attract many spectators. Hungary lost in the qualifying round in Wales in front of a record-breaking low number of spectators: 2,832.

2 // February

He was stocky and powerful—a man of action. Yet the most famous sentence in German soccer history can't seem to wait for him to act: "Rahn would have to shoot from a distance," exclaimed reporter Herbert Zimmermann, his voice emanating from millions of clanking transistor radios. Before listeners could even ask why Helmut Rahn didn't just shoot, the crescendo of the excited radio reporter declared: "Rahn's going for a shot!" The 3–2 win against Hungary in 1954 was a story that Rahn was asked to recount, over and over, for the rest of his life. That is, until he dropped out of public view—perhaps to avoid the same incessant question, but mostly due to business and health problems—long before his death in 2003. Yet he of all players, the man the people called the Boss, could have talked about any number of fabulous shots—for one, the six goals he scored in the 1958 World Cup. ⚽

1958 // Sweden

3 // February

> France's scorer Juste Fontaine (middle) leaves the Brazilian defense behind and stands alone in front of goalkeeper Gilmar.

< A seventeen-year-old Pelé chases down the ball.

Brazil's 1958 World Cup team put an end to the myth of unavoidable failure in soccer at the most critical moment. Indeed, the team's hard work created a new myth. In order to finally win the title, the players left nothing to chance, taking care of accommodations, getting used to the climate, and finding medical care early on. Even though, in the end, the enthusiasm over seventeen-year-old Pelé's five goals in the semifinal and final games got the lion's share of attention, this was a championship victory with all the makings of modern soccer; it was won on the basis of discipline and defensive work. Djalma and Nilton Santos were the best defensive duo in the world, and Gilmar was the best goalie in all of Brazil. Brazil played four games without conceding a single goal. It was only in the semifinal that Juste Fontaine was able to crack Brazil's defensive wall. In the end, however, Brazil won 5–2. ⚽

4 // February

Semifinal game Sweden vs. Germany, 60th minute: Erich Juskowiak was sent off the field for a retaliation foul. The atmosphere in Gothenburg was whipped up by "block wardens" calling out with megaphones. Reporter Gerd Krämer wrote: "Heya, heya. The hysterical cry of the fifty thousand spectators here today hangs in the air like the lid of an opium pot." Germany lost 1–3. In Germany, anti-Swedish sentiment erupted with an intensity not seen since the Thirty Years' War. On the Reeperbahn in Hamburg, there were signs saying, "Swedes are not welcome here." Gas station attendants refused to give gas to Swedes passing through, and tires on Swedish cars were slashed. At an equestrian event in Aachen, Sweden's flag was even taken from the mast. Restaurants removed the smorgasbord from all menus, and soccer burdened the relationship between the two countries. But after a few weeks, tensions eased. ⚽

5 // February

Substitute goalkeeper is a tough job: you have to wait until number one gets injured or falls out of favor. But there's a third option: to wait until the coach decides to protect the keeper from a confidence-dashing disgrace. This is how Heinz Kwiatkowski had the unexpected pleasure of guarding the German goal twice in the World Cup. In the 1954 qualifier against Hungary, the coach decided to let the second fiddle onto the field. The result? A 3–8 win for the East Europeans. And in the 1958 game for third place, when the German team was tired and frustrated and Juste Fontaine, the French force in front of the net, was pushing to settle accounts, the result was 3–6. Two World Cup games, fourteen conceded goals—the sad fate of a substitute goalie!

1958 // Sweden

6 // February

> Juste Fontaine cheers for France's third-place standing and is celebrated as the top scorer of the 1958 World Cup.
< The French goalie Claude Abbès clears a cross from the danger zone with a powerful punch.

Fontaine's fairy-tale world—his record will probably remain unmatched forever. With a four-goal tally in the game for third place, Juste Fontaine set the unprecedented record of thirteen goals in one World Cup. The Moroccan-born French citizen scored at least one goal in each of his six games, scoring eight times with his right foot, four times with his left, and once off a header. And yet, interestingly enough, this top scorer ended up on the French team thanks to the bad fortune of another: René Biliard had been injured shortly before the World Cup. ⚽

1958 // Sweden

7 // February

> Garrincha shows Swedes Sigvard Parling and Sven Axbom (from right) the meaning of Brazilian soccer wizardry.

< Sweden's goalie Karl Svensson clears the ball in front of Pelé (right).

Garrincha, "the Wren," called himself the Jungle Boy; his legs had been crippled by childhood paralysis. Finally, after many operations, the left leg was bent inwards and remained three inches shorter than the right, which bowed outwards. With these legs, he showed off the most amazing dribbling skills of all time. In a test against Florence before the World Cup, he outsmarted three defenders and the goalkeeper. One fake-out even caused a defender to jump against the goal post. He then guided the ball through the goalie's legs, tucking it nicely into the net. But at the World Cup, he not only made magic, but also fathered a little Swedish boy—one of his thirteen children with five women. Child support and drink proved to be his ruin. He died at the age of forty-nine in the slums of São Paulo. "No one will ever be able to dribble like Garrincha," said teammate Mario Zagallo. "He was the man who delivered the most joy in the history of soccer," wrote the Uruguayan poet Eduardo Galeano. ⚽

1958 // Sweden

8 // February

> Overcome with emotion after his stunning game, Pelé cries on Didi's shoulder. Orlando and Gilmar (from right) congratulate him.

< Brazil's Word Cup team on their lap of honor in Stockholm's Råsunda Stadium.

Gilmar, Djalma Santos, Bellini, Orlando, Nilton Santos, Zito, Didi, Garrincha, Vava, Pelé, Zagallo. No other team won a World Cup as convincingly as these men—they were perhaps the most exciting group of players ever to come together to kick the ball. And they boasted two natural wonders of soccer: Pelé and Garrincha. It was this truly Brazilian mix of zest for life, dancelike movements, love for the ball, athleticism, superstition, magic, readiness to attack, and a few incomparable players that turned football from the land of the samba into a new ideal of beauty. ⚽

1958 // Sweden

1962 // Chile

- 9 // February
- > 10 // February

Looking back on Chile in 1962, we're inclined to wonder whether the World Cup was paid for by the construction industry. The tournament was sometimes called the World Cup of Cement, other times the Bricklayer's World Cup. More and more, the childlike, playful joy of the game was giving way to an overly adult, even calculating approach: the fear of losing had finally exceeded the will to play. In this way, the 1962 World Cup in Chile was characterized by the unfavorable combination of excessive caution and overwhelming aggression. There were thirty injuries after only one-third of the twenty-four games in the qualifying round. With six players ordered off the field,

a new World Cup record had been set, although even more players should have been sent off, especially in the so-called Battle of Santiago between Chile and Italy. This all explains the low number of goals. Czechoslovakia scored three goals in four games, allowing them to pull into the semifinal. No other World Cup, save in 1934, has had such weak top scorers: whereas players normally needed six goals to be crowned top World Cup scorer, in 1962, no single player netted more than four. In contrast, only four years earlier, Fontaine (France) had scored thirteen. At least Brazil saved the aesthetic face of the game and took second place. There was a twenty-four-hour wait before the images of the games could be seen in Europe, since in those days there were no satellites for broadcasting the games live overseas. It wasn't until the reels had been delivered by plane that Europe could watch the World Cup on TV.

CAMPEONATO MUNDIAL DE FUTBOL
WORLD FOOTBALL CHAMPIONSHIP
CHAMPIONNAT MONDIAL DE FOOTBALL
COUPE JULES RIMET

CHILE
1962

// The Games

FIRST ROUND, GROUP A

Uruguay vs. Colombia 2–1
Soviet Union vs. Yugoslavia 2–0
Yugoslavia vs. Uruguay 3–1
Soviet Union vs. Colombia 4–4
Soviet Union vs. Uruguay 2–1
Yugoslavia vs. Colombia vs. 5–0

RESULTS
1. Soviet Union (Points: 5, Goals: 8–5)
2. Yugoslavia (4, 8–3)
3. Uruguay (2, 4–6)
4. Colombia (1, 5–11)

FIRST ROUND, GROUP B

Chile vs. Switzerland 3–1
Germany vs. Italy 0–0
Chile vs. Italy 2–0
Germany vs. Switzerland 2–1
Germany vs. Chile 2–0
Italy vs. Switzerland 3–0

RESULTS
1. Germany (Points: 5, Goals: 4–1)
2. Chile (4, 5–3)
3. Italy (3, 3–2)
4. Switzerland (0, 2–8)

FIRST ROUND, GROUP C

Brazil vs. Mexico 2–0
Czechoslovakia vs. Spain 1–0
Brazil vs. Czechoslovakia 0–0
Spain vs. Mexico 1–0
Brazil vs. Spain 2–1
Mexico vs. Czechoslovakia 3–1

RESULTS
1. Brazil (Points: 5, Goals: 4–1)
2. Czechoslovakia (3, 2–3)
3. Mexico (2, 3–4)
4. Spain (2, 2–3)

FIRST ROUND, GROUP D

Argentina vs. Bulgaria 1–0
Hungary vs. England 2–1
England vs. Argentina 3–1
Hungary vs. Bulgaria 6–1
Hungary vs. Argentina 0–0
England vs. Bulgaria 0–0

RESULTS
1. Hungary (Points: 5, Goals: 8–2)
2. England (3, 4–3)
3. Argentina (3, 2–3)
4. Bulgaria (1, 1–7)

QUARTERFINALS

Chile vs. Soviet Union 2–1
Yugoslavia vs. Germany 1–0
Brazil vs. England 3–1
Czechoslovakia vs. Hungary 1–0

SEMIFINALS

Brazil vs. Chile 4–2
Czechoslovakia vs. Yugoslavia 3–1

THIRD-PLACE MATCH

Chile vs. Yugoslavia 1–0

FINAL

Brazil vs. Czechoslovakia 3–1

World Cup Champion: BRAZIL

11 // February

The national stadium in Santiago de Chile was nicknamed the White Elephant due to the light color of the materials from which it was built. Erected in 1937, it was renovated for the 1962 World Cup and its capacity was doubled to 77,000 seats. Yet it wasn't the World Cup that turned it into a household name the world over, but rather the military coup of General Pinochet eleven years later. The stadium was used by the junta as a prison and torture chamber for thousands of political prisoners. This is why the Soviet Union refused to play against Chile in the national stadium in a 1973 World Cup qualifier (even though it had of course already been emptied of prisoners). So, in the end, eleven Chileans played against zero Soviets in front of 20,000 spectators. The fans cheered for a team that shot into an empty goal to qualify for the 1974 World Cup in Germany.

1962 // Chile

12 // February

> Big effort for zero goals: Germany's striker Uwe
Seeler (back) shoots, Italy's goalkeeper Lorenzo
Buffon dives, the ball lands out of bounds.
< The German and Italian captains, Hans Schäfer
(right) and Lorenzo Buffon, shake hands and
exchange pennants.

A new and more cautious approach to the game began to spread rapidly in the early 1960s. It was particularly evident in the Italian's *catenaccio* (door bolt), yet it was often combined with some very rough play. The match between Germany and Italy was in good company; one-sixth of the World Cup qualifiers ended without goals for either side.

1962 // Chile

13 // February

> Hungary's goalkeeper Gyula Grosics reaches
for the ball in the game between Hungary and
England in the qualifying round (final score: 2–1).
< Grosics secures the ball from Bobby Charlton's
attack (England, left).

Gyula Grosics participated in two more World Cups. But he, defender Jenö Buzánszky, and a seriously ill Puskás were the only members of Hungary's Wonder Team to witness the anniversary of the Miracle of Bern half a century later. Yet even so, many years afterward, Grosics—known as the Black Panther for his elegance—still had not gotten over the defeat of his life. As he admitted at a ripe old age, the defeat in the final game of the 1954 World Cup had haunted him every day since. "I always dream about it," said Grosics, who had been banished to the countryside by the Communist regime. "But even in the dream, we never win the final game."

14 // February

> Even Brazil's superb striker Pelé doesn't score a single goal in the o–o match against Czechoslovakia.

< Brazil's coach Moreira and Pelé.

At the age of twenty-one, four years after his sensational World Cup debut in Sweden, Pelé already was regarded as the wonder of the soccer world. Yet his second World Cup (like his third in 1966) didn't get off to an auspicious start. Following his goal in the 2–o game against Mexico, he suffered an injury to his thigh while attempting a shot against Czechoslovakia. He couldn't play for the rest of the tournament. The game ended o–o, and no one would have guessed that both teams would meet again in the final game. The only striker who could celebrate a success was the Czech Jósef Jelinek—not because he had scored a goal, but because of an announcement over the loudspeaker that he had just become a father. ⚽

1962 // Chile

15 // February

> Huge police presence in the national stadium in Santiago at the game between Italy and host Chile.

< Ken Aston, the only English referee at the 1962 World Cup, delivered the worst referee performance of the entire tournament.

"Referee to the phone": a popular call in German stadiums when the man in black doesn't appear up to his duties. It didn't ring for Ken Aston, though. The Englishman may lay claim to having overseen (or, as some would say, not seen) one of the most brutal World Cup games. Chile vs. Italy: from the beginning, hatred was at play. One reason was the fact that Italy had three players from Brazil and Argentina who had just become naturalized Italian citizens, a practice that struck the South Americans as unfair. Another was two prominent articles printed in the Italian press; Chileans had found the content quite insulting. The referee fueled this hatred by showing favoritism for the home team. By the end of the game, two Italians and no Chileans had been sent off the field—and Chile won 2-0.

> In a surprising change of style, the Italian defender Mario David (left) is more interested in the ball than his Chilean opponent Leonel Sánchez (No. 11).

< One of countless fouls: the Italian Sandro Salvadore, on the ground, doubles over in pain.

The press christened this disgraceful game the Battle of Santiago. Referee Ken Aston literally gave up in the face of such an "uncontrollable" match, as he called it. He sent the Italians Giorgio Ferrini and Mario David off the pitch, but not the Chilean, Leonel Sánchez, who had shattered Umberto Maschio's nose with a left hook in front of millions of viewers. It was such a brutal hit that people were left to wonder if they had tuned to the wrong sports channel on TV. If the rules had been followed, no fewer than two Chileans should have been suspended from the game. In any case, although Aston was signed up to ref other games following this one, the privilege was revoked. Despite all this, he ended up being put in charge of all referees in 1966, and was even promoted to top manager in 1970.

17 // February

> Uwe Seeler wins the ball in a showdown with Switzerland's Heinz Schneiter, subsequently heading it into the Swiss net. Germany wins 2–1.
< Hans Schäfer (Germany) in the qualifier against Chile.

To beat the host country in the World Cup is a difficult venture, and one that more often than not fails to meet with success. The home team has advantages: the fans, the conditions, and sometimes even the referee. In a truly artistic fashion, Germany pulled it off in 1962 for the first time with a 2–0 win over Chile, the first in a string of such wins. Victories over Spain in 1982, Mexico in 1986, and South Korea in 2002 followed. Beating the host nation four times constitutes a record, placing Germany ahead of the three won by Brazil—the only country that ranks ahead of Germany in other important statistics: the number of world titles and World Cup games won. ⚽

1962 // Chile

> Disappointment is written all over the face of Chile's goalie Misael Escuti just as Horst Szymaniak brings Germany into a 1–0 lead with a penalty kick.

< Friendly gestures: Herbert Erhardt (Germany) hugs his Chilean opponent after the final whistle is blown.

1962 // Chile

In 1906, goalies were prohibited from rushing the kicker in a penalty kick; in 1929, they weren't even allowed to move in front of the shot (a rule that wasn't recalled until 1997). The result was that their chances of blocking a penalty kick were minimal. As a result, forty-one out of forty-three penalty kicks made it into the goal from 1950 to 1970 at six World Cup tournaments. The goalies in 1962 had no luck whatsoever; every penalty kick landed in the net.

The Englishman Paul Gascoigne in the 1990s likened training players to raising chickens. He compared making a good chicken coop to instructing players on precisely controlled movements, strict rules, and fixed behavior that must be repeated exactly, always. And to be sure, having the players live together in the Hotel Belvédère in the Swiss town of Spiez helped Germany win the 1954 World Cup. It gave birth to the "spirit of Spiez"—a team unity that sprang from the "spirit of being roommates," as coach Sepp Herberger put it. However, in 1962 young professionals from the postwar generation began to join the team, bringing a new self-awareness with them. They wouldn't stand for being treated like mere recruits. Their frustration found an outlet when Hans Tilkowski trashed the team's living quarters in a military academy. Tilkowski had been assigned to substitute goalie, second to Wolfgang Fahrian. Needless to say, Germany didn't make it very far in Herberger's final World Cup. ⚽

> Brazil's Amarildo heads the ball into the net for the decisive goal, scoring his second goal in the 2–1 win in the qualifier against Spain.

< Eladio Rojas shoots the winning goal, putting Chile up 2–1 in the quarterfinal game against the Soviet Union.

One of the many enigmas in soccer is why a national team's success is not interchangeable with that of a club team. Spain had the best club team in Europe in the 1950s: Real Madrid. Yet the national team had no luck. It failed twice in qualifying for the World Cup (losing to Turkey in 1954 and Scotland in 1958). In 1962, the players finally made it and brought a near carbon-copy of Real Madrid with them, including a diverse sampling of different nationalities: Uruguayan-born José Santamaria; the former Hungarian Ferenc Puskás; Argentinean-born Alfredo di Stéfano; and the best-paid coach in the world and master of the defensive wall, the Argentinean Helenio Herrera. But di Stefano arrived injured and left with a sad record: he was the best player never to make it past group play. Spain fell through in the preliminary round.

1962 // Chile

"**In German stadiums**, bicycle kicks are rather rare," commented a soccer textbook in 1980. "The technique is easier for Latinos to perform, since they have a wider range of movement in the hips." The theory is bold, but history offers at least a few supporting arguments. The Chilean David Arellano was the first to show off the trick in Europe when his Colo-Colo club Leônides was hosted in Spain in 1927. And by all accounts it was, indeed, a work of art. In Brazil, Leônidas da Silva, the Rubber Man and 1930s star, made the bicycle kick famous. In Germany, the technique became widely known with Silvio Piola's famous bicycle trick goal in the match between world-champion Italy and Germany in 1938. In 1962 this artistic trick was still a rarity, and it has remained so to this very day. ⚽

22 // February

Pelé is considered the greatest player that Brazil has ever seen—and Garrincha the most popular. In 1958, the world was crazy about the seventeen-year-old Pelé, but it was Garrincha who left the Swedish defender standing in the right wing, setting up both of the final two goals for Brazil. And even if Pelé stands alone as a three-time world champion (eighteen players have won two titles), then this is mostly thanks to Garrincha. For when Pelé injured himself in 1962 in the second game and could only watch from the sidelines, Garrincha became the best player in the World Cup. He scored two goals in the quarterfinal against England and two in the semifinal against Chile. Even though he kicked the Chilean player, Eladio Rojas, and was ordered off the field, the officials didn't dare prohibit one of the most incredible players from participating in the final game—even if the rules dictated otherwise. ⚽

1962 // Chile

The Eastern bloc was never again as strong as it was during the World Cup of 1962. Preceded by the construction of the Berlin Wall and immediately followed by the Cuban missile crisis, this year represented the climax of the Cold War. Five of the sixteen participants and four of the eight quarterfinalists were countries located in the Soviet sphere of influence. But this didn't make them any more popular. The semifinal between Czechoslovakia and Yugoslavia took place in one of the most scenic stadiums in the world, the Estadio Sausalito, on a small tongue of land between the Green Lagoon and a piece of woodland in Vina del Mar, the Pearl on the Pacific. Yet this view wasn't enough for the public. While the other semifinal between Chile and Brazil in the packed national stadium in Santiago cast its spell over the entire country, the game between Czechoslovakia and Yugoslavia was the worst-attended semifinal in World Cup history, with a mere 5,890 spectators. ⚽

Since the 1990s, people have been talking about the globalization of soccer. Brazil, the largest source of raw materials for the art of soccer, exports many of its resources—nearly every talent and every star from Brazil ends up in Europe's richest soccer clubs. Yet this type of export has proceeded successfully only recently. Two stars from the world-champion team of 1958, goalie Vavá and key player Didi, were courted and transferred to Europe, Vavá to Atletico Madrid and Didi to Real Madrid, but neither of them achieved success in the Old World. Their art thrived only in their native surroundings. Due to shockingly high offers from Europe, Pelé was even declared by the government to be a "national treasure," a move that prohibited him from switching to a foreign team. He remained with his homeland club FC Santos for eighteen years. It was only with Romario, Rivaldo, and Ronaldo that a new generation of players spent nearly their entire careers in Europe. ⚽

25 // February

Modern sports photography can freeze the dynamics of competition in a split second, something that was made possible by the advent of the reflex camera in the 1920s. Yet for decades, the technology was still not good enough to zoom in on the action from very far away, in contrast to the focal lengths and fast shutter speeds of today's cameras. In 1962, South American photographers surprised European players and referees with their idea for solving this problem: during every time-out, they rushed out onto the field to snap pictures close up. The rush of reporters after the 2–1 win for Brazil in the final game was particularly heavy. Within seconds, top scorer Zito was surrounded by photographers, and his teammates and coach could barely get through to him. ⚽

26 // February

> Pelé (left), who couldn't play in the final game due to his injury, hugs his teammate Amarildo after Brazil wins the title.

< Captain Mauro holds the World Cup trophy in his hands.

Artur Friedenreich, son of a German immigrant and a black laundress, was Brazil's first soccer hero. He led the country to become South American champion in 1919. Shortly afterward, President Pessoa forbade all dark-skinned players from representing Brazil. In order to be able to play in clubs, they had to whiten their faces and slick back their hair. It took decades, but, finally, the soccer magic of black players became stronger than white racism. "This was the birth of the most beautiful playing style in the world, which consists of a bent upper body; the entire body swings all the while and the legs fly in a style that originates in Capoeira," an Afro-Brazilian martial art, wrote Eduardo Galeano of Uruguay. With their World Cup victories in 1958 and 1962, Brazil united all the many colors of soccer. ⚽

1962 // Chile

1966 // England

Long hair, short skirts, the music of the Beatles and the Rolling Stones—England was in the middle of the swinging sixties. And the swing spread to the World Cup as well, which was being hosted in the sport's original home in honor of the one hundredth anniversary of the English Football Association and, thus, of the game of soccer. For the first time, the World Cup had a mascot, a kicking lion named World Cup Willie. Yet it was another four-legged friend who became the first national hero: a dog named Pickles. The World Cup trophy, the Coupe Jules Rimet, had been stolen before the tournament from a postage stamp exhibition in London. One week later, while being taken for a walk, the black-and-white spotted mongrel dug up a package in someone's front yard—and, lo and behold, it was the World Cup trophy! The country was relieved and Pickles became famous overnight. Four months later the trophy was officially placed in English hands: after the dramatic final victory over Germany, Captain Bobby Moore was finally able to present the beer-bottle-sized piece of gold to admiring crowds, putting an end to a one-hundred-year dry spell for the country that invented soccer. This topped off a tournament in which the previous world champions, Italy and Brazil, made fools of themselves; the newcomers North Korea and Portugal made names for themselves; the Europeans accused the South Americans of foul play; the South Americans complained about the European referees—and in which probably the most disputed goal in soccer history would decide the tournament.

// The Games

FIRST ROUND, GROUP A

England vs. Uruguay 0–0
France vs. Mexico 1–1
Uruguay vs. France 2–1
England vs. Mexico 2–0
Uruguay vs. Mexico 0–0
England vs. France 2–0

RESULTS
1. England (Points: 5, Goals: 4–0)
2. Uruguay (4, 2–1)
3. Mexico (2, 1–0)
4. France (1, 2–5)

FIRST ROUND, GROUP B

Germany vs. Switzerland 5–0
Argentina vs. Spain 2–1
Spain vs. Switzerland 2–1
Germany vs. Argentina 0–0
Argentina vs. Switzerland 2–0
Germany vs. Spain 2–1

RESULTS
1. Germany (Points: 5, Goals: 7–1)
2. Argentina (5, 4–1)
3. Spain (2, 4–5)
4. Switzerland (0, 1–9)

FIRST ROUND, GROUP C

Brazil vs. Bulgaria 2–0
Portugal vs. Hungary 3–1
Hungary vs. Brazil 3–1
Portugal vs. Bulgaria 3–0
Portugal vs. Brazil 3–1
Hungary vs. Bulgaria 3–1

RESULTS
1. Portugal (Points: 6, Goals: 9–2)
2. Hungary (4, 7–5)
3. Brazil (2, 4–6)
4. Bulgaria (0, 1–8)

FIRST ROUND, GROUP D

Soviet Union vs. North Korea 3–0
Italy vs. Chile 2–0
North Korea vs. Chile 1–1
Soviet Union vs. Italy 1–0
North Korea vs. Italy 1–0
Soviet Union vs. Chile 2–1

RESULTS
1. Soviet Union (Points: 6, Goals: 6–1)
2. North Korea (3, 2–4)
3. Italy (2, 2–2)
4. Chile (1, 2–5)

QUARTERFINALS

England vs. Argentina 1–0
Germany vs. Uruguay 4–0
Portugal vs. North Korea 5–3
Soviet Union vs. Hungary 2–1

SEMIFINALS

Germany vs. Soviet Union 2–1
England vs. Portugal 2–1

THIRD-PLACE MATCH

Portugal vs. Soviet Union 2–1

FINAL

England vs. Germany 4–2 OT

World Cup Champion: ENGLAND

1 // March

Soccer makes music. Or, more precisely, its fans make the music. Especially in English arenas, a rich repertoire of spectator songs and rhythmic cheers has developed since the 1960s. Thanks to international broadcasts, some of the hits have spread throughout the entire world, including the legendary "You'll Never Walk Alone," which the fans of FC Liverpool took from the song of the same name by the band Gerry and the Pacemakers in 1963. By the time Liverpool pulled off a sensational Champion League success in 2005, it had become a perennial favorite. In 1966, the British stadium singers appropriated the so-called "soccer rhythm" from the hit "Hold Tight" by Dave Dee, Dozy, Beaky, Mick & Tich, which spread across the globe thanks to the World Cup and today is sung in nearly every stadium.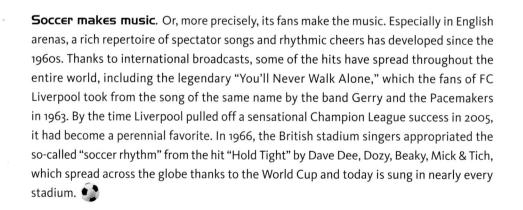

2 // March

The English Disease is what people twenty years later would call the brutality of hooligans who used the games as a way to spread fear. After their behavior led to a disaster with thirty-nine deaths in the Heysel Station at Brussels in the 1985 European Championship game, stadiums increasingly became high-security affairs, designed to ensure that such tragic events would never happen again. The stadiums of the twenty-first century are set up with surveillance cameras that can zoom in on and identify each spectator. But looking back, this photogenic scene says more than the thousands of pictures taken with modern surveillance: here, unarmed bobbies stand around in the stadium. One of them takes a souvenir snapshot, thus creating exactly what this picture here is: a document of a forgotten past. ⚽

3 // March

The Packed Defense—a tactic of highly organized backline defense invented before the war by the Swiss Karl Rappan and called *riegel* (door bolt or defensive wall). This technique was perfected by the Italians, who called it *catenaccio*. Yet the Swiss defense of 1966 proved to have as many holes as a piece of Swiss cheese. This was undoubtedly due to the fact that the key players Jakob Kuhn, Leo Eichmann, and Werner Leimgruber went for a "pub crawl with the ladies" on the night before the first game. Not surprisingly, the head manager Alfredo Foni kicked them off the team. Switzerland then proceeded to suffer a terrible 0–5 loss to Germany. The team subsequently proved itself to be anything but a band of brothers and fell apart, losing to Spain and Argentina. It would be Switzerland's last chance at the World Cup for twenty-eight years.

4 // March

> Left: Giacinto Facchetti (Italy). Right: The Uruguayan Pedro Rocha beats goalkeeper Marcel Aubour, bringing Uruguay up to 1–1 in the qualifier Uruguay vs. France (2–1).

There had been only four different world champions up until 1966, and 1966 proved a success for only one of them: Germany. The other three said their good-byes prematurely and had to deal with the hostile reception awaiting them in their home countries. Title-defender Brazil was eliminated following defeats to Hungary and Portugal. Italy had to swallow the disgrace of a century when it lost to North Korea. And Uruguay, which at least made it to the quarterfinals, attracted attention mostly because of its fouls, finishing behind Germany 0–4 after two players had been sent off the field.

5 // March

> The World Cup newcomers from North Korea celebrate their sensational 1–0 victory over two-time world-champion Italy.

The United States' 1–0 victory over England in 1950 was the first big sensation in World Cup history. It was the first time that the motherland of soccer had deigned to send its professional players to the World Cup, so it was particularly humiliating when the team ended up losing to a group of amateurs that had been more or less tossed together. Joe Gaetjens, a Haitian dishwasher working at a German restaurant in New York, shot the winning goal. Then, sixteen years later, along came a young soldier named Pak Doo Ik, who weaseled the ball away from star player Gianni Rivera and shot the winning goal for a 1–0 North Korean victory over Italy—and thus, World Cup history had witnessed its second sensation of the century. "The Fall of the Roman Empire has nothing on this!" wrote *Northern Echo.*

6 // March

> Brazil's star Pelé is fouled roughly in the qualifier against Portugal (1–3). Next to him: the Portuguese Eusébio (left) and the English referee George McCabe.

< At the beginning of the World Cup, Pelé is still able to have a good laugh.

Title-holder Brazil had good reason to complain about its elimination. It was especially painful for Pelé, the best player the world over, who had been brutally fouled in the first game by the Bulgarian Dubromir Zhechev. He was sidelined in the game against Hungary, only to be injured so seriously by the Portuguese João Morais that he could only limp along. Because substitutions still were not allowed at that point, Brazil had absolutely no chance. At the time Pelé declared that he never wanted to play another World Cup again (but reconsidered things later). Yet it was another player who became the scapegoat for Brazil's defeat: goalkeeper Manga, who had made a mistake by coming out of his goal in the game against Portugal. He suffered an especially humiliating form of revenge: his name became part of the vernacular in Brazil. For a long time afterwards, a mistake committed by a goalkeeper was called a *mangueirada*.

> Team captains Ignacio Zoco (left) and Uwe Seeler shake hands before the group game Spain vs. Germany (1–2).

< Spain's goalkeeper José Iribar takes a goal kick.

Shaking hands, exchanging pennants, wishing the opponent a good game—the usual formalities before the first whistle is blown. But in one respect, it was the World Cup newcomer North Korea, of all countries, that brought confusion to the program. National anthems normally are struck up before the games while the teams are standing in rank and file. And it was precisely this minor detail that caused such embarrassment. Because England didn't maintain diplomatic ties to the communist regime in Pyongyang, the bands weren't allowed to play the North Korean national anthem. The organizers were confronted with a real dilemma and decided to make a clean sweep in the standard protocol. They simply prohibited all national anthems from being played. Upbeat marches were performed instead. It was only after North Korea had been eliminated in the quarterfinals that national anthems were played for all. ⚽

8 // March

Soccer players need talent not only to play but also to stay healthy. At least for a long career, the ability to recover quickly is indispensable. The best example is Uwe Seeler, the German captain in 1966, who played in all four World Cups from 1958 to 1970. He played more than 1,400 games over the course of his career and suffered more than one hundred injuries. He had eight operations, surviving all of them—including the most difficult one: surgery to repair a tear in his Achilles tendon. In the mid-1960s, this was an accident that cost many players their careers. Not so for Seeler. Only seven months after tearing his tendon, he scored the decisive goal in 1965 for Germany's World Cup qualification with a 2–1 victory over Sweden. ⚽

9 // March

It's not all that common for the names of soccer players to be immortalized. For this to happen, they need to have accomplished something unique. And on July 20, 1966, in Birmingham, England, Lothar Emmerich did just that: in the 39th minute he tucked the ball into the top of the net with his left instep, shooting from just outside the box at an extremely sharp angle. Since then, a goal made from an "impossible" angle like this is called an "Emmerich goal" in German soccer jargon.

10 // March

> A listless play in the group round: Germany vs. Spain. Horst-Dieter Höttges, Willi Schulz, and Franz Beckenbauer (from left).
< Beat on the ground: Spanish defenders after Uwe Seeler's 2–1 winning goal.

If there has always been a secret favorite in the World Cup, then it has been Spain. The team had always been looked upon highly. But it was always eliminated prematurely due to a combination of bad luck and poorly timed mistakes. The fact that Spain could never win as a national team, even though it had the most successful clubs for fifty years in the European Championship, has been attributed by experts to the strained relations between central Spaniards, Catalan, and Basques. As the theory goes, these tensions worked their way into their game. In 1966, Spain was under the rule of the soccer fan Franco, who placed great emphasis on soccer in his Nationalization agenda. Yet despite the sideline runs of the legendary left wing Francisco Gento—the only player to win the European Championship six times (with Real Madrid)—Spain lost this time as well to Argentina and Germany.

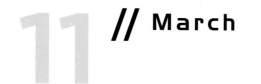

11 // March

Fans, officials, photographers, and marching bands—all types of people fill up the soccer field before the game starts. Yet when the referee blows his whistle, the field belongs to the players alone. At least that's what we'd like to think. In South America in the 1960s, a different idea prevailed. The line between the observers and the observed was not all that clear. This was never more apparent than during Chile's games, during which a photojournalist from this South American country used nearly every time-out to rush out onto the field in order to be closer to the action. In his country, this was normal at that time. In Europe, however, people found this behavior unacceptable. Because the man couldn't leave well enough alone, he finally was escorted from the field by English police officers.

12 // March

The Uruguayan Horacio Troche would end up putting an entirely new spin on the tradition of the captains' handshake. Before the quarterfinal game against Germany, he still shook hands in traditional fashion. But when he was sent off the field in the 49th minute for kicking Lothar Emmerich in the lower abdomen, he wanted to give Seeler a fitting farewell: he boxed his ears. The German didn't do him the favor of hitting back, thus sparing himself the fate of being sent off the field. Five minutes later, Hector Silva also was ordered off the field, and Uruguay lost 0–4.

13 // March

> "Kaiser Franz": Franz Beckenbauer, only twenty years old, in the quarterfinal game against Uruguay.
< Uwe Seeler and his opponent Horacio Troche (right).

In 1966, his nickname Kaiser Franz had not yet been coined. Yet at twenty years of age, Beckenbauer was offering glimpses already of how majestic and light on his feet he could be. Indeed, the Munich-born member of the German team was the discovery of the World Cup in England, where he shot four goals from midfield. The only players who had scored more goals in the tournament were the strikers Eusébio with nine and Helmut Haller with five. The French sports newspaper *L'Equipe* declared Beckenbauer in 1994 one of the three best players in World Cup history, surpassed only by Pelé and Maradona.

1966 // England

14 // March

> The Uruguayans Julio Cortez (left) and Luis Ubinas attempt to placate the English police rushing by.

< Hector Silva (left) refuses to leave the field; the police have to remove him by force.

South America felt cheated by Europe in 1966. Brazil felt that its star, Pelé, wasn't being protected enough against the malicious fouls of the European defenses. Argentina felt that it was at a disadvantage in the 0–1 game with England because of the German referee, who had ordered their captain Antonio Rattin off the field. In their 0–4 loss to Germany, Uruguay felt the same about the English referee, who sidelined Horacio Troche and Hector Silva. The result was a climate of heightened tension between both great soccer continents, which was especially apparent in the only regular comparison: the so-called World Championship between the winners of the continental club competition. These matches became all the more brutal after the 1966 World Cup, until Europe withdrew in 1973, no longer interested in playing against such violent opponents. ⚽

15 // March

In 1966, the atmosphere and architecture of the English arenas fired up crowds from all corners of the earth. England had secured its reputation as the mecca for soccer fans. Yet the layout and atmosphere of the stadiums also harbored a risk: they were crowded, tight, and the mood was always intense. This became obvious twenty-three years later when a tragic disaster befell spectators at Hillsborough Park in Sheffield, which had served as the venue for three World Cup games, including the quarterfinal game between Germany and Uruguay. At an English championship semifinal game in 1989, ninety-six spectators were killed in a mass panic in the overcrowded, fenced-off grandstand of Sheffield Hillsborough Stadium. The tragedy prompted a new approach to stadium design. Ever since, stadiums have been built almost exclusively with fence-free seating.

16 // March

Nearly forty years later, referee Rudolf Kreitlein could still remember the most exciting scene of his career as a referee: the gigantic Argentinean Antonio Rattin stood before him, over a foot taller than the Swabian master tailor, and refused to leave the field after having been ordered off. For seven minutes. At the end of the brutal quarterfinal, the English coach Alf Ramsey forbade his players to exchange their jerseys with "those animals" in front of the queen. The South Americans felt that Kreitlein had cheated them of a fair game, and for his own safety Kreitlein had to be escorted from the field by the police. Even in the German victory over Uruguay, there were problems with removing two South Americans from the pitch. Later, while he was waiting at a traffic light, the referee manager Ken Aston had the inspired idea of using bright yellow and red cards to make the referees' intentions clear, regardless of the player's native language. They were first used in 1970. ⚽

17 // March

The power and powerlessness of the collective: in nearly all team sports, the Soviet Union reached the top—in handball, basketball, volleyball, and, in particular, in ice hockey, but never in soccer. The superpower achieved its best results at the 1966 World Cup in the semifinals with a team heavily outfitted with players from Moscow clubs. Later, in the 1980s, the USSR team was adapted more to the Ukrainian model, led by the legendary coach Valeri Lobanovsky, who had expanded upon the Total Soccer of Holland— a style of play that relied upon each player's ability to play every position, which allowed players to confound opponents by constantly changing positions on the pitch. Under Lobanovsky's direction, the team blossomed but lost in 1986, even with their well-played game. In 1988 they won second place in the European Championship, as well as the Olympic gold medal. Yet with the fall of the Soviet Union, this collective fell as well. ⚽

> Franz Beckenbauer (right) sails over a leg stuck out by a Russian opponent.
< Lothar Emmerich one-on-one with Galimizjan Khusainov (front).

A World Cup under the shadow of foul play: there has always been intentional rough play in soccer, but in England it reached a critical mass. Defenders would rush the opponent, and their intentions were often all too obvious: injuring the opponent could produce a winning advantage. At the time, substitutions still were not allowed. If a player who wanted to injure his opponent could deliver the blow skillfully enough, it was more likely that the opponent would be injured than that the aggressor would be sent off the field. In order to stem the tide of fouls, the system of yellow and red cards was introduced in the next World Cup. And, finally, teams were allowed to substitute players—as they had been able to do in club soccer for quite some time. From this point on, players had a lot more incentive to kick the ball rather than their opponents. ⚽

19 // March

1966 // England

Vladimir Nabokov didn't only write *Lolita*, he wrote about his personal experiences in soccer as well: "I was crazy about goalkeeping. In Russia and the Latin countries, that gallant art had been always surrounded with a halo of singular glamour." He was quoted elsewhere as saying, "The goalkeeper is the lone eagle, the man of mystery, the last defender. Less the keeper of a goal than the keeper of a secret." But in this position, nice saves count for more than nice words. And so it was not Nabokov who became the most famous goalkeeper in the world, but rather his Russian compatriot Lev Yashin.

20 // March

When France became world champion in 1998 with a team composed of players from all five continents, it became clear that the former colonial empires had changed the face of European soccer. The teams from England, Belgium, and Holland also increasingly reflected the multicultural diversity of their populations—a positive development for the culture of the games. Yet as early as the 1960s, Europe already had seen its first star among the colonial kickers, as the first soccer star from Africa, the Mozambique-born Eusébio, shined with Benfica Lissabon and Portugal's national team. In 1966, he led Portugal to third place in the country's first ever World Cup and became the top scorer. He scored four of his nine goals in the 5–3 win over North Korea in the quarterfinal, bringing his team up from a 0–3 deficit earlier in the game.

21 // March

The first championship final as a television event: for most people, the 1954 and 1958 World Cups were events to listen to on the radio. And in 1962, the tournament was in Chile and thus too far away for Europeans to experience it live. But 1966 was a different story. According to official estimates, roughly 400 million viewers in fifty-two countries were sitting in front of their TVs when the opening whistle was blown—more than a tenth of the world's population at the time! The viewers would not come to regret it: this was perhaps the most exciting final game in World Cup history. ⚽

1966 // England

> During the entire tournament, he let only three balls slip by: the English goalkeeper Gordon Banks.

< This bobby isn't exactly flashing a smile at the camera.

The zero has to stay: with these words, the founding tactical model of successful soccer was formulated for the people. Yet the importance of the zero after the hyphen, the "to zero" final score, had become clear already in the 1960s. While the World Cups in the previous decade offered lots of wild scoring frenzies (the record being in 1954, with 5.38 goals per game), the statistic froze in 1962 and 1966 at the "modern" number of 2.78 goals per match. In soccer, caution had taken command. Since then, the prevailing philosophy has been that you win spectacular games with your offense, but you win the important ones—big titles, in other words—with your defense. England set the example in 1966: goalkeeper Gordon Banks conceded only one goal before the final game. ⚽

23 // March

> The German striker Siegfried Held (right)
eludes the English defender George Cohen.
< English fans in the Union Jack look.

England was the motherland of the legendary wings Stanley Matthews and Tom Finney. However, after their retirement, England won its first World Cup title in 1966 with what came to be known as the Wingless Wonder formation. With his popular and successful tactics, coach Alf Ramsey anticipated certain shifts in modern soccer. He played without wings, having defenders Ray Wilson and George Cohen assume their responsibilities instead. At the same time he strengthened midfield to achieve superiority there—also a characteristic of modern soccer. And he played Nobby Stiles as a "sweeper" in front of the defense. Even today, the position of the sweeper between defense and midfield is one of the most critical in the game.

24 // March

> Wolfgang Weber (middle) forces overtime with his equalizer in the 90th minute for a score of 2–2.
< Germany's goalkeeper Hans Tilkowski punches a ball out of the danger zone.

Headers aren't the only thing in soccer that make human hardware and software grind and pop. That's why Nobby Stiles, son of a gravedigger and well-known for his rough play, had the wise habit of leaving his teeth in the locker room. This made quite an impression on England's opponents and saved on repair costs. Wolfgang Weber was made of tough stuff, too. The defender from Cologne is best known for the equalizer he shot for Germany in the final minute of the championship final. Lesser known is the fact that he played with a broken leg once in an association match. As he later recounted, he checked the stability of the cracked bone during halftime by jumping from the bench onto the ground. The bone hurt, but held, and so Weber played on. ⚽

25 // March

> To call or not to call? No question for Bobby Charlton (left) and the top scorer Roger Hunt (far right), who plead for the referee to call the goal, which would bring the score to 3–2. On the ground: German goalkeeper Hans Tilkowski.

< Ready to make decisions: the Soviet linesman Tofik Bakhramov.

The Wembley goal, the most famous goal that wasn't: it decided the 3–2 game for England in the 1966 World Cup final. Geoff Hurst's shot in overtime banged against the underside of the crossbar, crashed onto the ground, and from there bounced back out onto the field. When it hit the ground, was it behind or in front of the line? Goal or no goal? What thereafter ensued became perhaps the most famous dialogue in the history of soccer. The Swiss referee Gottfried Dienst asked the linesman Tofik Bakhramov, "Was the ball behind the line?" The linesman nodded clearly, saying, "Yes, behind the line," and pointed toward the middle. A scientific analysis conducted by Oxford University in 1995 came to the conclusion that the ball had not been inside the goal. ⚽

26 // March

"They think it's all over!"—these would become legendary words in English sports reporting. As Kenneth Wolstenholme spoke into the microphone, spectators already were running onto the field. But at that very moment, Hurst shot another goal, bringing England to a 4–2 lead. "It is now," the reporter concluded. While England celebrated, one of the losers, Helmut Haller, snatched the ball and took it with him in the general confusion, even though the rules state that the ball goes to the referee at the end of the game. Haller didn't cough it up until thirty years later, just before the start of the European Championships in England, when the English were searching for the ball from their greatest soccer day ever. ⚽

Does the right belief help win the game? The German theologian Joachim Staedtke wrote a thirteen-page "Report on an Ecumenical Soccer Game Between Catholic and Evangelical Theology Through the Ages." It ended in a 1–1 draw with goals by Martin Luther and Thomas Aquinas. In reality, however, the score is 13–4 for the Catholics, if not more. Thirteen of the seventeen World Cups up until 2002 were won by Catholic countries from South America and southern Europe. And three of the four other World Cup victories are debatable—Germany, for one, which is half Protestant, half Catholic. Only one world champion made it to this position without papal assistance: the English Anglicans in 1966.

> The English team captain Bobby Moore holds the trophy high.

< Queen Elizabeth II presents Bobby Moore with the Coupe Jules Rimet.

1966 // England

After the World Cup trophy had been stolen, the heroic dog, Pickles, sniffed out the trophy for the World Cup in someone's front yard, sparing England an embarrassment. As a reward, Pickles was allowed to follow the opening game of the World Cup from the VIP box. Shortly afterward, he tragically met his end, strangling himself with his own leash while chasing a cat. But his previous efforts proved worthwhile for his team: after the final game, Captain Bobby Moore had the honor of accepting the delicate gold trophy from the white-gloved hands of the queen. ⚽

1970 // Mexico

Mexico 1970 stands a cut above all other World Cups in two respects: it showcased not only the best and most thrilling victor, but also the most dramatic game. Brazil and its star Pelé conjured up magic that no one had expected, considering the heat and high altitude—but that was precisely why they succeeded. The conditions simply didn't allow the Europeans to rely on their usual advantage: stamina. Brazil went on to win its third World Cup. Thus, in accordance with FIFA rules, the Coupe Jules Rimet, given out since the first World Cup in

1930, was placed in Brazil's hands for good. The small, delicate trophy, which had been lost in England in 1966, only to be discovered by the dog Pickles shortly thereafter, was then stolen once again. Only this time there was no happy ending: the gold statue ended up being melted down by its captors. Ever since, only a replica exists. A copy of the replacement trophy was presented for the first time in 1974, which, at over 10 pounds, was much heavier and larger than the original. The name of the winning country is engraved into the base of the trophy, and there is enough space for names until 2038. But it was not the best team that offered the best game of the World Cup—it was Italy and Germany. They delivered such a dramatic, indeed mythical, performance in the semifinal that this game has been dubbed by many the Game of the Century.

// The Games

FIRST ROUND, GROUP A

Mexico vs. Soviet Union 0–0
Belgium vs. El Salvador 3–0
Soviet Union vs. Belgium 4–1
Mexico vs. El Salvador 4–0
Soviet Union vs. El Salvador 2–0
Mexico vs. Belgium 1–0

RESULTS

1. Soviet Union (Points: 5, Goals: 6–1)
2. Mexico (5, 5–0)
3. Belgium (2, 4–5)
4. El Salvador (0, 0–9)

FIRST ROUND, GROUP B

Uruguay vs. Israel 2–0
Italy vs. Sweden 1–0
Uruguay vs. Italy 0–0
Sweden vs. Israel 1–1
Sweden vs. Uruguay 1–0
Italy vs. Israel 0–0

RESULTS

1. Italy (Points: 4, Goals: 1–0)
2. Uruguay (3, 2–1)
3. Sweden (3, 2–2)
4. Israel (2, 1–3)

FIRST ROUND, GROUP C

England vs. Romania 1–0
Brazil vs. Czechoslovakia 4–1
Romania vs. Czechoslovakia 2–1
Brazil vs. England 1–0
Brazil vs. Romania 3–2
England vs. Czechoslovakia 1–0

RESULTS

1. Brazil (Points: 6, Goals: 8–3)
2. England (4, 2–1)
3. Romania (2, 4–5)
4. Czechoslovakia (0, 2–7)

FIRST ROUND, GROUP D

Peru vs. Bulgaria 3–2
Germany vs. Morocco 2–1
Peru vs. Morocco 3–0
Germany vs. Bulgaria 5–2
Germany vs. Peru 3–1
Bulgaria vs. Morocco 1–1

RESULTS

1. Germany (Points: 6, Goals: 10–4)
2. Peru (4, 7–5)
3. Bulgaria (1, 5–9)
4. Morocco (1, 2–6)

QUARTERFINALS

Uruguay vs. Soviet Union 1–0 OT
Italy vs. Mexico 4–1
Brazil vs. Peru 4–2
Germany vs. England 3–2 OT

SEMIFINALS

Italy vs. Germany 4–3 OT
Brazil vs. Uruguay 3–1

THIRD-PLACE MATCH

Germany vs. Uruguay 1–0

FINAL

Brazil vs. Italy 4–1

World Cup Champion: BRAZIL

31 // March

This is the top: two years after hosting the Olympics, Mexico also served as the venue for the World Cup, here at the opening ceremony in Aztec Stadium, 7,350 feet above sea level. Hosting both world events consecutively was unprecedented.

1970 // Mexico

1 // April

> The Mexican team at the opening celebration, minutes before their opening game against the Soviet Union (0–0).

< National coach Helmut Schön in the German Soccer Association's VW Beetle.

The 1970 World Cup was a colorful event, so it is only fitting that Mexico's opening game against the Soviet Union (0–0) was the first to be broadcast on color TV. But this was not the only thing that made the game special. It was also the first time a yellow card was handed out, or that players could be substituted. During a break, Anatoli Pusatch replaced his teammate Albert Shesterniev, ensuring that Pusatch would at least have his own footnote in the annals of soccer history. Many teams used new tactical maneuvers that were made possible by the new rule allowing substitutions—Germany with "the Joker" Grabowski, for example. Not permissible before 1966, substitutions were conceived originally as a way to replace injured players. But, of course, they immediately were employed as a tactical element. ⚽

The stage was now clear for the leading actor: the ball. In the picture shown here, Peru's players make friends with it, just to be on the safe side. At this point, it still cost the lives of a few head of cattle, because the ball that was used in the World Cup was still made of leather. Only during the 1970s did use of leather decline, slowly making way for synthetic materials that were cheaper, more uniform in performance, and required less maintenance. And the synthetic ball didn't absorb rain like its leather cousin, so it maintained a constant weight. The German firm Adidas was the first to produce the ball in 1970, and has produced all World Cup balls since—with constantly updated, market-friendly designs. In Mexico, there were two models for all contingencies: Telstar, in the classic black and white design (or entirely white in games played under floodlights), and Chile (made from brown, natural leather for hard, dry fields).

3 // April

> **Germany's top scorer Gerd Müller, with a hat trick in the qualifier against the Bulgarian Asparuch Nikodimov's team (right).**

"Short, fat Müller" is what coach Tschik Cajkovski initially called the young lad from northern Germany who had transferred to the up-and-coming FC Bayern Munich team. The short, round young man would never comment on the moniker, but answered instead in his own personal language: with goals. At the World Cup in 1970, the whole world finally could catch a glimpse of this unbelievable goal-scoring talent. In the opening game against Morocco, Müller saved the German team with the winning goal for a 2–1 finish. Then, against Bulgaria, he scored three times for a score of 5–2 (also in the picture: the overtaxed defender Asparuch Nikodimov). And this was just the beginning! ⚽

4 // April

1970 // Mexico

"The moments of the great outside forward, those were moments of freedom," waxed the German theater critic Peter Iden in 1980. The glory days of this position were the 1950s and 1960s, when players would run up the sidelines, kicking up clouds of chalk. Yet in 1966, England became world champion without them—coach Alf Ramsey pulled the classic outside forward positions into midfield with numbers 7 and 11. Playing right and left forward thus became a dying art. That last unforgettable game played with outside forwards was Germany's 5–2 win over Bulgaria, in which Reinhard Libuda ran circles around the defense. A bribe scandal in the national league would ruin his career later. After this, Libuda was never again able to gain a foothold in life. Impoverished and addicted to alcohol, he passed away in front of his television set at the age of fifty-three.

5 // April

> Alberto Gallardo (Peru) in the qualifier against Germany (1–3).

< Gerd Müller in the Peruvian jersey.

A change of clothing, but too late: Alberto Gallardo wears the Peruvian jersey with the thick, red diagonal stripe and the V-neck, a real fashion classic in soccer history, for the ninety minutes of the game. After the final whistle, he exchanges jerseys with his opponent, Gerd Müller (small picture). Undoubtedly, the Peruvians wished that the players had exchanged jerseys before that, because Müller scored all three goals in their 1–3 defeat— wearing his German jersey, of course.

6 // April

A school portrait for a class of its own: the Brazilian team, which presents itself here before the World Cup in 1970 during practice in white and blue, already was used to turbulence. Shortly before the World Cup, coach João Saldanha was fired, allegedly following a command from the higher-ups. The military rulers in power since 1964 had it out for this well-known socialist—not only because of his political views, but also his choice of players. As rumor had it, Saldanha had wanted to leave Pelé at home. In the end, Saldanha stayed at home himself. Mario Zagallo (far left in the picture), who had played for both world championship-winning sides in 1958 and 1962, took over. After seven spectacular games, he finally had cause for celebration: he was the first person to become world champion as both player and coach. ⚽

7 // April

....

....

....

....

Clear the way! Gordon Banks is shown here during one of his powerful goal kicks, which flew even farther than normal in the thin air of the high altitudes. The qualifying game against Brazil in 1970 would be the last for this 1966 World Champion goalkeeper. He pulled off an unforgettable save, blocking a header by Pelé. Banks had to sit out the quarterfinal game due to an intestinal problem, but without him, England was eliminated. It was only twelve years later that England again managed to qualify for a World Cup. Banks of England, so named for his proverbial stalwartness, didn't concede any goals in thirty-five of seventy-three international matches. This is a record that no other goalkeeper in the entire world has surpassed. Over the course of his career, he kept a clean sheet nearly 50 percent of the time. ⚽

8 // April

In England, two events in particular from 1970 endure in the collective memory of the nation. They weren't goals, but rather examples of superb defensive work against Brazil's Pelé in the qualifier: a legendary save by goalkeeper Gordon Banks and an artistic tackle by defense leader Bobby Moore. England ended up winning 1–0. For Moore, however, it was a mess of a World Cup. The captain of the title defender couldn't tap into his normal stash of top-class skill—the result of four days spent in a Colombian jail for allegedly stealing a jeweled bracelet. It later proved to be a hoax by conmen who used tricks like this to blackmail prominent figures. Moore's innocence was eventually restored, but his World Cup form was spoiled. ⚽

9 // April

The Aztec Stadium in stereo: the hallucinatory effect created here with a photographic montage taps into a widespread fear that the difficult playing conditions in Mexico might pose a threat to the players' health. The thin air of the high altitudes, which ranged from just over 5,000 feet in Guadalajara to roughly 8,800 feet in Toluca, and the blazing summer heat of the high-afternoon sun (many of the games began at noon because this was optimal for broadcasts to Europe) were both causes for worry. Yet in the end, the conditions didn't cause the physical breakdowns that had been feared; the players adapted their game to the environment. They ran less and more slowly, and let the only entity that could stand the high altitudes and the heat do the work. As Sepp Herberger said, "The ball is in the best condition."

10 // April

A new breed of defenders began to populate the fields in the early 1970s: the offensive defenders. They played the outside right or left, but instead of just waiting for the other team's wings to approach, they would attack as well when the opportunity presented itself, forcing their way up the sideline, thus taking over the wing's role. Such players included the likes of Terry Cooper (right)—not to be confused with the 007 actor of the same name in the James Bond parody *Casino Royale* (1967)—here in the quarterfinal game between Germany and England. Another offensive defender was Hans-Hubert Vogts, although it goes without saying that his name is in no danger of being confused with 007.

11 // April

> Beside himself: England's goalkeeper Peter Bonetti has to come to terms with the 2-2 draw; Uwe Seeler has just scored.

< Uwe Seeler's (right) legendary header with the back of his head.

Approximately one out of every five goals is scored off a header, but a header has never been declared by spectators to be the "goal of the year." And it's no wonder, because goals shot using the feet tend to be more spectacular. According to the books, to have the best chance of actually netting a header, you have to use your forehead. But the greatest and most memorable goal scored with a header was executed with a different part of the skull: in the 1970 World Cup quarterfinal, Uwe Seeler headed the ball past a baffled goalkeeper (Peter Bonetti) with the back of his head—the equalizer that brought Germany up 2–2, paving the way into overtime and finally a victory over England. It became the most famous header goal in German soccer history. ⚽

1970 // Mexico

12 // April

The Heat Wave of Léon and the point at which it boiled over: Gerd Müller scored the winning goal for Germany during an action-packed overtime in which possession volleyed dramatically between the two teams, putting Germany up for a final score of 3–2. It was the first time England had given up a 2–0 lead in an international match in ninety-eight years.

13 // April

Why did England lose? Because coach Alf Ramsey substituted out the tired, slave-driving Bobby Charlton? Or because of Montezuma's revenge? That perennial malady of visitors to Mexico—intestinal problems—forced the legendary Gordon Banks to trade in his standard position in the goal for a seat on the toilet. His substitute, Peter Bonetti, was unable to rise to the occasion. He let Franz Beckenbauer's shot through, along with Seeler's header. An English book published in 1998, *What If?*, claims that if England had won the title, Prime Minister Harold Wilson wouldn't have been voted out and Britain would have been spared "Iron Lady" Margaret Thatcher and her tough politics. So a goal—or more precisely, intestinal trouble—can indeed change the world.

1970 // Mexico

14 // April

> Franz Beckenbauer (left), here still with a healthy shoulder, and Gianni Rivera in the Game of the Century, Italy vs. Germany.
< Goalkeeper Sepp Maier and striker Gianni Rivera, the scorer of the 4–3 winning goal.

Italy vs. Germany, the Game of the Century. Or at least the overtime of the century. This semifinal had all the mythical elements that make for an unforgettable game. The dramaturgy of the Italians' lead early on in the match; German sprints at the high altitude; Enrico Albertosi's saves; Beckenbauer's imperial elegance coupled with his heroic grace, which allowed him to play with a torn shoulder, his arm in a sling following Giacinto Facchetti's foul; the time running out for Germany, their faith fading fast—and then, a miracle: Karl-Heinz Schnellinger scores an equalizer in the 90th. ⚽

15 // April

"**Schnellinger, of all players,**" yelled the German TV reporter over and over after Germany's equalizer in the game against Italy—of all people, the defender who had played in the Italian league and in forty-seven international games for Germany scored only this one time. And then: overtime. Even goalkeeper Sepp Maier sprinted across the entire field to hug his teammate, whose late draw blessed the spectators with the best overtime of all time.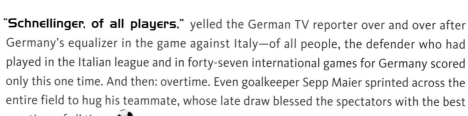

16 // April

Out of all the scenes from the so-called Game of the Century, it is the image of an injured Beckenbauer that has survived more than any other—why did he, of all people, have to be injured? None other than the philosopher Martin Heidegger had praised his invulnerability. His shoulder injury came after Germany already had substituted two players, so without Beckenbauer, they would have had to play with only ten men. With an improvised brace, his chest and upper arm slung together like a mummy, Beckenbauer played on with one arm—and absolutely unforgettable grandeur. This picture shows a hero who could only have been prevented from forging ahead by being dragged off the field; with his hand on his heart, he refuses to leave his teammates. It was a touching expression of an individual's capacity for suffering, a quality that was rewarded by an eternal place in public memory and the lasting status of a hero. ⚽

> **The last hope for the final game: Gerd Müller's (Germany) header in overtime secures a 3–3 draw.**

1970 // Mexico

Müller once again: in overtime, the German top scorer executed a true work of art against the Italian masters of defense, putting Germany up 2–1—he stole a ball the Italians thought was safe, threaded it through the legs of the defender and goalkeeper, and tucked it into the net. Later in the game, Italy was up 2–3, but Müller scored an equalizer with a header. A young offensive talent in Brazil by the name of Luis Antonio Correa da Costa was impressed by the German scorer—so much so that in the 1980s, once he had become a professional player and was on the national team, he assumed the stage name Müller, even though the umlaut over the "u" doesn't exist in his native language. ⚽

18 // April

> Tarcisio Burgnich, who scored the goal to bring Italy up to 2–2, and Pierluigi Cera (right), as Italy celebrates its win.

< In commemoration of a memorable game: Giacinto Facchetti (left) and Gerd Müller exchange jerseys.

The ninety-minute *catenaccio* was cracked by Schnellinger at the last minute—and followed by an intoxicating overtime full of goals. Müller's goal; Burgnich's equalizer; 3–2 for Italy as Berti Vogts lets Luigi Riva run; a second equalizer by Müller; finally Rivera shoots the winning goal for a 4–3 finish. A game like no other. The Italian author Romano Giardini wrote in his *Reasons to Love the Germans* (1996), "White and *azzurri* (light blue) are not opponents, but rather interpreters of an opera, like the Montagues and Capulets in a soccer rendition of *Romeo and Juliet,* when the ball was still classically leather-toned." ⚽

Müller doesn't score a single goal: a one-time occurrence in the 1970 World Cup. In the match for third place, Wolfgang Overath beat Uruguay's elegant goalkeeper Ladislao Mazurkiewicz for the winning goal, banking a 1–0 finish in Germany's favor. But with ten goals, Müller was the top striker and a new international star. Only two players ever had scored more goals in a World Cup tournament, both in the minimal-defense days of the 1950s: in 1954, the Hungarian Sandor Kocsis (eleven goals), and in 1958, the Frenchman Juste Fontaine (thirteen goals). In 1974, the Pole Grzegorz Lato tallied seven goals, and Müller only scored four. But the German still had cause for celebration: the fourth in the net was the winning goal for the World Cup title. In the next six World Cups, up to 1998, no single player managed to score more than six goals. It was only in 2002 that Ronaldo came close to Müller's record by landing eight. The Brazilian is the only active player who poses a threat to Müller's world-record total of fourteen World Cup goals—Ronaldo has twelve to date. ⚽

20 // April

The man of a thousand goals. Pelé scored what was allegedly his thousandth goal in 1969 with a penalty kick. It is a number that statisticians are skeptical about (a more realistic estimate would be between five hundred and eight hundred). Yet it is undeniable that Pelé, like no other, represented the perfect combination of energy, athleticism, and elegance in his game. In the game against Italy, he tucked a header into the net, bringing Brazil up 1–0 and laying the foundation for Brazil's third World Cup victory. Pelé had been there for all three of them.

> The South American artistry against European brute strength: Clodoaldo (left) man-on-man with Luigi Riva.

Felix, Carlos Alberto, Brito, Wilson, Everaldo, Clodoaldo, Gerson, Jairzinho, Tostao, Pelé, Rivelino: for many, these eleven names signify the best soccer team ever to have played. Six games, six wins, each more beautifully played than the last. Talent, team spirit, the heat, and the high altitude worked to the advantage of Brazil's artistic approach—and to the disadvantage of the Europeans' power-oriented style. Nothing was to be won by running alone; the players had to let the ball run its own course. Brazil turned this maxim into a crowning achievement with the last goal of the World Cup for a 4–1 final victory over Italy. Each of the eleven players touched the ball before it rolled over to captain Carlos Alberto in the right half. He then rushed forward, driving the ball at shoulder-height into the left corner of the goal.

22 // April

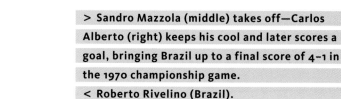

> Sandro Mazzola (middle) takes off—Carlos Alberto (right) keeps his cool and later scores a goal, bringing Brazil up to a final score of 4–1 in the 1970 championship game.
< Roberto Rivelino (Brazil).

By making it to the World Cup final game for Italy, Sandro Mazzola had reached the crowning point in his family history—it would have made his father proud. Valentino Mazzola was the captain of the legendary team AC Turin, which made up almost the entire Italian national team, before it was wiped out in a plane crash in 1949 near Turin. Sandro Mazzola, who was six at the time, became one of the best players in the world, following in his father's footsteps.

23 // April

> Recognition without envy: Italy's goalkeeper Enrico Albertosi congratulates Pelé on his well-earned victory.

< Jairzinho is celebrated by Brazilian fans.

Picasso defined modern art as "freedom with order." But some feel that too much order is threatening to suffocate the freedom of the modern art of soccer. "Today's soccer is fenced in by systems," commented the Brazilian Mario Zagalo in the 1990s. As a player in 1958 and a coach in 1970, he was a part of possibly the two most exciting teams in soccer history. "The systems," he continued, "prevent the players from expressing their individuality. This is something we have to fight against." But in 1970, rigid systems were not necessarily prevailing over the freedom of individual players. For example, Italy's old masters of defensive strategy were powerless against the solo artistry of players like Jairzinho, who shot a goal in every World Cup game, and the incomparable Pelé. ⚽

When Brazil lost the World Cup in 1950 to Uruguay in Rio de Janeiro, the uniforms were accused of being accomplices in the defeat: the white jerseys with blue collars were seen as too unpatriotic. A competition to design a new national uniform was announced. The requirement: it had to have all the colors of the Brazilian flag—yellow, green, blue, and white. Out of three hundred contestants, the nineteen-year-old Aldyr Garcia Schlee won: yellow shirt, green collar, green cuffs, blue shorts with white stripes, and white socks. In 1958, the year of their first World Cup victory, the players weren't allowed to wear the uniform because their opponent in the final game, Sweden, was wearing yellow. In 1962, they finally had their first World Cup success in yellow. For the viewing public, however, 1970 was the first year that Brazil celebrated in color, since it was the first World Cup to be broadcast on color TV. ⚽

1974 // Germany

There were only sixteen teams this year, even though Australia, Central Africa, and the Caribbean were represented for the first time. In Europe and South America, this meant that there was even more competition for a spot. Countries like England, France, Spain, and Portugal fell by the wayside in the qualifying rounds. The World Cup boasted an incredible diversity of colors, but it certainly could have used a bit more first-class soccer. Superior skills were contributed by two countries that hadn't participated in the World Cup since 1938: Holland and Poland. They played their best games but lost narrowly to world champion Germany. In truly dramatic fashion, the World Cup host had lost a landmark duel to East Germany in the preliminary round, but this political setback turned out to pave the way to the title. Because of this defeat, West Germany was matched against weaker opponents in the final round by virtue of a new system that saw the championship final immediately follow the final round. (This system replaced the knockout system with quarter- and semifinal games.) Thus, two years after a shining European Championship victory, West Germany was able to prove itself once again—only this time with slightly less refined means. In a repeat of the World Cup twenty years earlier, West Germany pulled off a final victory over technically superior opponents with the help of stereotypical German virtues: unity, determination, fighting spirit, and physical conditioning.

WM 74

13. 6. – 7. 7. 1974

Hamburg   Düsseldorf   Frankfurt
West - Berlin   Gelsenkirchen   Stuttgart
Hannover   Dortmund   München

Fußball-Weltmeisterschaft 1974

// The Games

FIRST ROUND, GROUP A

West Germany vs. Chile 1–0
East Germany vs. Australia 2–0
West Germany vs. Australia 3–0
East Germany vs. Chile 1–1
Australia vs. Chile 0–0
East Germany vs. West Germany 1–0

RESULTS
1. East Germany (Points: 5, Goals: 4–1)
2. West Germany (4, 4–1)
3. Chile (2, 1–2)
4. Australia (1, 0–5)

FIRST ROUND, GROUP B

Brazil vs. Yugoslavia 0–0
Scotland vs. Zaire 2–0
Yugoslavia vs. Zaire 9–0
Scotland vs. Brazil 0–0
Scotland vs. Yugoslavia 1–1
Brazil vs. Zaire 3–0

RESULTS
1. Yugoslavia (Points: 4, Goals: 10–1)
2. Brazil (4, 3–0)
3. Scotland (4, 3–1)
4. Zaire (0, 0–14)

FIRST ROUND, GROUP C

Holland vs. Uruguay 2–0
Sweden vs. Bulgaria 0–0
Bulgaria vs. Uruguay 1–1
Holland vs. Sweden 0–0
Holland vs. Bulgaria 4–1
Sweden vs. Uruguay 3–0

RESULTS
1. Holland (Points: 5, Goals: 6–1)
2. Sweden (4, 3–0)
3. Bulgaria (2, 2–5)
4. Uruguay (1, 1–6)

FIRST ROUND, GROUP D

Italy vs. Haiti 3–1
Poland vs. Argentina 3–2
Argentina vs. Italy 1–1
Poland vs. Haiti 7–0
Argentina vs. Haiti 4–1
Poland vs. Italy 2–1

RESULTS
1. Poland (Points: 6, Goals: 12–3)
2. Argentina (3, 7–5)
3. Italy (3, 5–4)
4. Haiti (0, 2–14)

SECOND ROUND, GROUP 1

Holland vs. Argentina 4–0
Brazil vs. East Germany 1–0
Brazil vs. Argentina 2–1
Holland vs. East Germany 2–0
Argentina vs. East Germany 1–1
Holland vs. Brazil 2–0

RESULTS
1. Holland (Points: 6, Goals: 8–0)
2. Brazil (4, 3–3)
3. East Germany (1, 1–4)
4. Argentina (1, 2–7)

SECOND ROUND, GROUP 2

West Germany vs. Yugoslavia 2–0
Poland vs. Sweden 1–0
Poland vs. Yugoslavia 2–1
West Germany vs. Sweden 4–2
West Germany vs. Poland 1–0
Sweden vs. Yugoslavia 2–1

RESULTS
1. West Germany (Points: 6, Goals: 7–2)
2. Poland (4, 3–2)
3. Sweden (2, 4–6)
4. Yugoslavia (0; 2–6)

THIRD-PLACE MATCH

Poland vs. Brazil 1–0

FINAL

West Germany vs. Holland 2–1

World Cup Champion: WEST GERMANY

27 // April

> > A young Brazilian inspects the German World Cup mascot.
>
> < The opening ceremony in the Frankfurt Wald Stadium: hundreds of people on the pitch come together to present the official World Cup logo.

Is this what soccer players in Europe look like? Tip and Tap at Sugarloaf Mountain in Rio: the country hosting the World Cup sends both of its mascots to the nation of the incumbent World Cup champions. ⚽

1974 // Germany

28 // April

> Dull performance by incumbent world-champion Brazil in the opening game: Jairzinho (left photo, right) in a header duel and Leinvinha, who just misses Enver Maric's (Yugoslavia) goal.

< After participating four times from 1958–1970, Pelé merely observes from the grandstand for the first time.

Null ouvert is a popular tactic in the national card game of Germany known as skat. But when the zeroes were as wide open as in the opening game of 1974, the German fans in the stadium also blew the whistle. Pelé, who retired from the world champion team after the 1970 World Cup—first to become a journalist, later to promote Afri-Cola in Germany—looked on in boredom as his teammates disappointed with a 0–0 draw against Yugoslavia. ⚽

29 // April

> Chile's goalkeeper Leopoldo Vallejos takes his eye off the ball just once, but this is enough to concede the game to Germany.
< Chilean soccer fans protest against the military regime in their country.

Looking back at the goal often only reminds the goalkeeper of the ball that got away. This was no exception for the Chilean Vallejos, who in this picture studies the ball's last flicker of life after Breitner's goal put Germany up 1–0. The host's first game was also a politically controversial match. At first, there were protests about hosting the game in the divided city of Berlin. Then, protests by Chilean spectators broke out against the military dictatorship in their country. And Chile, after the coup against the Allende government, made it to the 1974 World Cup without a fight. It just so happens that the Soviet Union refused to appear in the eliminator, which was held in the national stadium in Santiago, where the Chilean military regime had confined and executed political dissidents. So only eleven Chileans and the referee stood on the field. They shot into an empty goal and the game was over: Chile had qualified. ⚽

> Australia's defenders Manfred Schaefer and Doug Utjesenovic (both in the air, from left) clear the ball in front of Jupp Heynckes (far left) and Gerd Müller.

< The Germans Uli Hoeneß and Gerd Müller against Australia's Peter Wilson and goalkeeper Jack Reilly (from right).

Australia at the World Cup: it was the sparsely populated fifth continent's debut, after having beaten the team from the most populous continent, Asia, in the qualifying round. But Australia didn't stand a chance against either of the German teams. They lost to East Germany 0–2 and to West Germany 0–3, where the clinical finisher Gerd Müller scored the third goal. The last names of the defenders who tried in vain to stop him—Schaefer and Utjesenovic—are proof that soccer in Australia was still a game of European immigrants and their descendants, and not a national sport like football, rugby, or cricket. ⚽

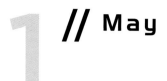

1 // May

> One of West Germany's many chances against the World Cup newcomer Australia: Uli Hoeneß heads the ball over the opponent's goal.

His blond shock of hair shone like a halo, yet Uli Hoeneß wasn't able to ascend to real goal-scoring success against Australia on his own. Nevertheless, despite many lost opportunities, this favorite team had an easy game and qualified early for the final round—even before the politically loaded third qualifier against East Germany.

1974 // Germany

> The fans of the team from Zaire also prove to be fans of the dictator Mobutu Sese Seko.

< Mantantu Kidumu, Zaire's captain.

Central Africa—a continent that made an appearance on the world stage of soccer for the first time in 1974. The fans from Zaire (today the Democratic Republic of Congo), with their yellow and black clothes, also celebrated the dictator Mobutu Sese Seko. Were they acting under orders? As it turns out, there wasn't much to rejoice. Zaire lost 0–2 to Scotland, 0–9 to Yugoslavia, and 0–3 to Brazil. The self-proclaimed "leopards" turned out to be nothing more than harmless kittens. African soccer still had a long way to go—and African democracy even farther. ⚽

3 // May

> Johan Cruyff (left), here man-on-man with the Uruguayan Juan Masnik, is considered one of the best players of all time alongside Pelé, Beckenbauer, and Diego Maradona.
< Dutch fans at the Holland vs. Uruguay qualifier (2–0).

1974 // Germany

Total Soccer makes its debut. It was developed in Holland, a former no-name in the soccer world, and took on a new dimension in the 1970s as the more attack-heavy game we know today. Players with continually changing positions, techniques, and speed—and right in the middle of it all, the greatest player of his generation: Johan Cruyff, the key player for the European champion Ajax Amsterdam. ⚽

4 // May

> Luigi Riva (right) takes off and shoots past the goal. If Italy had played Haiti with as much skill as did Poland, whose team trashed the Caribbean nation 7–0, the players would have spared themselves a tomato shower.

< The Italians Gianni Rivera (left) and Luciano Spinosi.

Soccer players toil on foreign soil to bring joy to their fans back home. Unfortunately, however, the fans don't always appreciate how difficult this can be. In their 3–1 opening victory over Haiti, Italy's players couldn't have guessed that, in the end, just two little goals would prevent them from progressing to the next round. How were they to know that their elimination would spawn a repeat of 1966, when they were eliminated in the qualifying round and were greeted upon their return home with a deluge of tomatoes? But for at least one of Haiti's players, the World Cup would lead to something even worse. Ernst Jean-Joseph was the first player in the World Cup to be convicted of taking drugs. As punishment, he was locked in his hotel room by the Haitian secret service, beaten up, and taken back to his country like a prisoner, where the wrath of the dictator François "Papa Doc" Duvalier awaited him. ⚽

5 // May

The Caribbean cracks the catenaccio: a twenty-two-year-old kid from a slum in Port-au-Prince became the first star of this World Cup. Italy, the second-place finisher in 1970, hadn't conceded a single goal in twelve years. But then the team played against Haiti, the first Caribbean team to participate. "Exotic" was the buzzword used to refer to these teams—another word for hopeless. But then Emmanuel Sanon sprinted through the Italian defense and circled past goalkeeper Dino Zoff—1–0, what a sensation! The reporters were stunned. Hectic calculations followed: it turns out that Zoff's running streak of zero goals conceded had come to an end after a total of 1,143 minutes—still the world record for international games. Haiti lost 1–3, didn't stand a chance against Poland and Argentina, and wasn't able to qualify again. Yet to this day the country still lives off of the excitement of Sanon's goal.

6 // May

In the early years of soccer, players were more reserved when they celebrated a goal. Scorers hopped around a bit, shook hands, and that was it. Over time, however, success-ful plays gained more expressive after-plays. By the 1974 World Cup, they had become the stage for innovative forms of celebration. We have Poland to thank for this development. Indeed, it is a country that has found numerous opportunities to practice its cheers. As the real surprise success in 1974, the team scored sixteen goals in the tournament—more than any other team. And there was something entirely new to see after these goals: kisses among men. The heartfelt smackers for scoring teammates, especially for the top-scorer Grzegorz Lato, became a familiar sight. After an increasing number of teams started to adopt this custom, it became a touch too quaint for the traditionally minded FIFA. So in 1981 it introduced rules to punish celebratory kisses, which it felt were too "unmanly" and "excessively emotional." ⚽

7 // May

More than just a game: Germany vs. Germany. West Germany vs. East Germany. This awkward encounter took place only once during the forty years that Germany was a divided nation: on June 22, 1974, in Hamburg. What a strange twist of fate that the two countries ended up playing against each other in the only World Cup in which East Germany would ever participate! ⚽

1974 // Germany

8 // May

"**When I die**, if all they write on my gravestone is Hamburg '74, everyone will know that it's me lying there," said Jürgen Sparwasser many years after the evening on which his name would be immortalized in both East and West Germany. Of course, bitterness also played a role, because he felt burdened by the way in which his government exploited him politically as part of the conflict between the East and West. In 1988, Sparwasser defected to West Germany. The blue GDR jersey he had exchanged with Paul Breitner in Hamburg after the game in 1974 in the locker room hallway—East German players weren't allowed to do this in front of the cameras—was auctioned off to benefit flood victims when the Oder River burst its banks in 2003. Since then, the famous jersey has been kept in the Historical Museum in Bonn. ⚽

1974 // Germany

9 // May

> Gerd Müller (middle) in a race for the ball with the East German players Bernd Bransch (left) and Hans-Jürgen Kreische.

< Jürgen Sparwasser jumps over goalkeeper Sepp Maier in the direction of Franz Beckenbauer.

"Why We Will Beat the 'GDR' Today" was the title given to a cover story presented by *Bild,* the largest West German tabloid. In keeping with their customary usage, "GDR" was set in quotation marks, demonstrating a lack of recognition for East Germany as a sovereign state. But the uninspired home team, which had qualified already for the final round, didn't get anywhere, despite its total of thirty-one shots over East Germany's fourteen. The guests won 1–0 in a sensational game, and the prophets of victory in the struggle between political systems had a problem. *Bild* circumvented the issue with a clever distraction, launching an attack on their own national coach with the headline: "Not like that, Herr Schön!" ⚽

1974 // Germany

10 // May

> A spellbound Jürgen Sparwasser (right) watches the ball, unaware that this goal will go down in German soccer history as the Sparwasser Goal.

< The numbers on the scoreboard were a surprise for everybody in the Hamburg Volkspark Stadium.

VOLKSPARKSTADION HAMBU
DDR — BR DEUTSCHLAND
1 : 0
SPARWASSER 14

1 : 0

"On June 22, 1974, at 9:03 p.m., a shot rang out that shook West Germany. No, not from guns at the border between East and West Germany or from the Red Army Faction, but rather in the Volkspark Stadium in Hamburg," wrote Thomas Blees in his book *90 Minutes of Class Struggle,* which, twenty-five years later, tells the story of the Germany vs. Germany game. The reaction to Jürgen Sparwasser's winning goal in the media was quite varied in 1974. In the West, the defeat in Hamburg trumped all other topics and was treated as adisgrace—embarrassing because the players from "over there" (the East Germans) could now celebrate themselves as the "better Germans," as the news magazine *Stern* put it. In the East, however, the main topic in *Neues Deutschland* was National Construction Workers' Day. ⚽

11 // May

More than just a winning goal: after its victory, the East German team celebrated in front of its following, which was exactly 1,303 members strong. These fans had been sent into "enemy territory" in Hamburg, West Germany, to toe the party line, and had been selected especially by the East German State Security Service, the infamous Stasi. The requirements: they had to be married and had to "prove their steadfastness in the ideological struggle against imperialism." Yet sweet victory on the political front proved to be bitter medicine athletically: a draw would have allowed East Germany to avoid the difficult final group round with Brazil, Argentina, and Holland. The East Germans didn't stand a chance against those powerhouse teams. In contrast, their defeated cousins in the West easily worked their way into the final game, having been pitted against lesser opponents in the group round: Yugoslavia, Sweden, and Poland. ⚽

> Jairzinho (left) and Americo, the Brazilian
team's masseur and witch doctor.
< Brazilian fans are in a good mood after their
3–0 victory over Zaire.

The Brazilian masseur Americo had something of the magic of a medicine man in him. He didn't just knead muscles and mix tonics—he nursed souls. In addition to tears and bruises, he also chased away evil spirits. For 45 years, Americo was the witch doctor of the Brazilian national team. With a boxer's build, not a hair on his head, and two permanent sidekicks (a plastic bucket and a leather belt with balms and ointments), he was an unmistakable phenomenon in soccer. "You have to talk to the injury; it's 90 percent psychology," he would say. In this way, the Brazilian massaged his team to the World title three times. After his seventh World Cup in 1974, Americo retired from his job and started another: as a representative in São Paulo's parliament. ⚽

13 // May

> Goalkeeper Muamba Kazadi and Boba Lobilo
(above, both Zaire) with their total defense.
< Kazadi in flight.

1974 // Germany

Can you find the Brazilian in this picture? Zaire's defenders around goalkeeper Muamba Kazadi are in the majority as they vie for the ball, much to the dismay of their besieged opponent. Three against one, the Africans might have stood a chance. But eleven against eleven they were up a creek, as was to be expected against the world champions. The Africans lost 0–3.

14 // May

> The art of photography with soccer artists: a futuristic man-on-man in the qualifier Zaire vs. Brazil 0–3.

< A female fan wrapped in the Brazilian flag.

Soccer for the futurists: the photographer's blur technique freezes the energy of running players in a single moment, blending different levels of color and distorting the ball, turning it into a rough, shapeless object. It transforms the game into a work of art with dynamics that crisscross the picture, like the works of Umberto Boccioni—the Italian futurist.

15 // May

People in Haiti may be familiar with voodoo. But the fact that the Olympic Stadium in Munich was almost as empty as a ghost town during this game didn't help the players from the Caribbean island. Argentina won 4–1 and, thanks to the goal difference with Italy, made it to the final round. Unfortunately, the empty stadium was hardly the exception. While many soccer fans have had a tough time getting tickets for the World Cup to be held in Germany in 2006, it seems that German spectators in 1974 were only interested their own team's matches—and maybe those of Brazil, too. Other than that, the only games to achieve a large head count in 1974 were those involving Holland and Italy—thanks to the followings these countries were able to bring with them. The other qualifying matches didn't even fill half of the World Cup stadiums.

1974 // Germany

16 // May

The founding of a soccer temple: only two of the nine World Cup stadiums were built especially for the event. One of them, the Gelsenkirchen Park Stadium, only survived for twenty-eight years before it had to make way for the roofed Schalke Arena. The new Westphalia Stadium in Dortmund, however, became an unprecedented success and has survived to this day. As the only stadium built solely for soccer, without a track around the pitch, it brought spectators closer to the events than ever before and became a model for numerous other arenas. Opened in 1974 with 54,600 seats, within thirty years its capacity had increased to 82,000, making Borussia Dortmund the most well-attended club in Europe, with an average of nearly 80,000 spectators per game.

17 // May

> A celebration in orange, disappointment in red: the Dutch team congratulates itself on its 4–1 victory over Bulgaria.

< Johan Cruyff in the Dutch national uniform.

Soccer orange: Johan Cruyff and his vassals set the colors of the World Cup. Or, more exactly, their followers did. At Holland's six games in the preliminary and final rounds in Hanover, Dortmund, and Gelsenkirchen, tens of thousands of Dutch day-trippers turned German streets the color of the House of Orange-Nassau. At the World Cup, however, it became the color of King Johan—Johan Cruyff. ⚽

1974 // Germany

18 // May

> Lothar Kurbjuweit (East Germany) is impressed with Brazilian break dancing à la Luis Pereira.

< Luis Pereira wants to exchange jerseys with the East German goalkeeper Jürgen Croy—but he needs it for the next few games.

Ball art as a call to dance: Luis Edmundo Pereira and Lothar Kurbjuweit were ahead of their time. The Brazilian's high-leg number anticipated break dancing in the 1980s, and Kurbjuweits's hopping around heralded the casual disco style of John Travolta in 1977.

Hardly anyone could kick a soccer ball as hard as Roberto Rivelino. In his early days as a street soccer player he once shot the ball so hard it rendered his opponent unconscious. This fate would have befallen his teammate Jairzinho in 1974 had he not gotten to the ground quickly enough, a feat with which he luckily had had enough practice. "I kicked the ball so well that I could have seriously injured him," said Rivelino. The East German players were amazed that Jairzinho was suddenly standing among them in the free-kick defense; pleasantly surprised by his friendly help in protecting socialism, they gladly made room for him. But then Rivelino shot and Jairzinho dropped to the ground in a fraction of a second. To the amazement of the East Germans, the spot where Jairzinho had stood only moments before was suddenly wide open, and the ball whizzed through, slamming into the net for the winning goal. The cunning free-kick idea had worked. And thus Roberto Rivelino was the first man ever to find the hole in the East German wall. ⚽

20 // May

> Wim Suurbier (left) and Roberto Perfumo in the second round: Holland vs. Argentina 4–0.
< Argentina's goalkeeper Daniel Carnevali takes a goal kick.

Play low, win high: an old soccer adage that Holland took to heart in 1974. The Dutchmen were particularly light on their feet in their first win in the final round against Argentina. With their 4–0 finish, they quickly became a World Cup favorite—not bad for a new face that had been eliminated in the qualification for the European Championship ten years earlier in a defeat to Luxembourg. ⚽

What's the opposite of a Pyrrhic victory? There's no equivalent metaphor for a (tactical) defeat that turns out to be a (strategic) victory in the end. But with the 0–1 defeat to the East German guests, the West German host team was placed in the easier group in the final round. The defeat was also a loud wake-up call for the West Germans: national coach Helmut Schön was, at least informally, deprived of all authority, and captain Franz Beckenbauer, with his teammates from Bayern Munich, took over the command. With newfound drive and the goals of the Bavarians Breitner and Müller, Germany secured a 2–0 victory over Yugoslavia. ⚽

22 // May

Yugoslavia was one of only four European teams to participate in the first World Cup in 1930. Besides them, only the French, Belgian, and Romanians dared undertake the weeklong voyage to distant Uruguay in the winter. They all were traveling on the same ship, so the teams eliminated earlier had to wait around until the last passengers were ready for the journey back: the Yugoslavians, that is, who had reached the semifinal. Despite their incredible game and ball control, this was a onetime success story for the Balkan players with the exception of 1962, when they took third. They always lost to the powerhouse German team just before the semifinals: 1954, 1958, and 1974, here with a 0–2 loss in Düsseldorf. ⚽

1974 // Germany

23 // May

> No chance for the Yugoslavian Dragan Dzajic (middle): Berti "the Terrier" Vogts and Sepp "the Cat from Anzing" Maier have been keeping their eyes peeled.

Football fans love their animals: their nicknames make up a veritable zoo on the field. In the 1960s, goalkeeper Lev Yashin was called "the Black Spider," and the superb striker Eusébio "the Black Panther." In Germany, Willi Lippens was called "the Duck" and Franz Roth "the Bull." In England, the long-necked Jack Charlton was coined "the Giraffe." And even the name "the Flying Pig" wasn't meant as an insult to Tommy Lawrence, but rather as praise for the impressive agility of this heavyweight goalkeeper. In 1974, two faithful pets looked out for the German team: defender Berti Vogts (left), nicknamed "the Terrier," and goalkeeper Sepp Maier, "the Cat from Anzing," helped keep a clean sheet. ⚽

1974 // Germany

24 // May

Thirty years later, a new arena with a sliding roof was built on the same spot—but in 1974, spectators were still at the mercy of the elements in the yet-uncovered Rhine Stadium in Düsseldorf. A total of 68,000 spectators, most of them with only umbrellas to protect them from the unrelenting rain, experienced the most action-packed—and wettest—game of the World Cup: West Germany vs. Sweden, which ended 4–2. ⚽

1974 // Germany

25 // May

> What amounted to a game of water polo in Frankfurt's Wald Stadium: Gerd Müller (right) makes sure that the West German team isn't washed up in the final round with his goal against Poland.

< Groundskeepers try in vain to gain control of the water.

1974 // Germany

Rain is a German's—or at least a German soccer player's—best friend. In 1954 at the World Cup in Bern, the pouring rain left the ground in a soggy state that gave the Germans, with their power-oriented playing style, an advantage over the technically superior Hungarians. In 1974, the rain created a slippery playing surface that made for a dramatic victory for West Germany in the match against Sweden. Three days later, in the decisive game for entry into the championship final against Poland—a team known for its offensive strength—cloudbursts transformed the Frankfurt playing field into a swamp on which a game centered around good ball control was nearly impossible. Poland, which desperately needed a win, was at a disadvantage—their otherwise fluid offensive game got stuck in the mud. Gerd Müller put an end to this water polo match with his goal, securing a final score of 1–0 for West Germany. ⚽

26 // May

> 1–0 in the first minute: Johan Neeskens brings Holland into the lead with a penalty kick.
< Goalkeeper Sepp Maier kicks the ball; next to him: Johan Cruyff (Holland).

It was the quickest of all final goals. Not a single West German had touched the ball, but there it stood, already stuck in the net. After the kickoff, Johan Cruyff had taken off with the ball. Vogts tried to mark him but couldn't keep up. Then Hoeneß stuck his leg out—which meant a penalty kick for Holland. And in a flash, Johan Neeskens pummeled the ball with full force right into the center of the goal. ⚽

1974 // Germany

27 // May

The final duel of the World Cup stars: Franz Beckenbauer turns away, Johan Cruyff jumps into thin air; the West German sweeper gets to the ball first and kicks it into goalkeeper Sepp Maier's arms.

28 // May

Whoever leads 1–0 always loses—this soccer superstition has its roots in the history of World Cup final games. In all five finals from 1950 to 1966, the team who first took the lead ended up losing. In 1970, this pattern was broken by Brazil, only to resume in 1974 when Holland conceded its 1st-minute lead after goals by the West Germans Breitner and Müller. But that was the end of this particular superstition. Since 1974, every team that has first taken the lead in the final game has also won the world title. ⚽

29 // May

> Wolfgang Overath (West Germany, right) one-on-one with Wim Suurbier (Holland).
< Rainer Bonhof (left) against Johan Neeskens (Holland).

Why did Holland lose the championship final in 1974? This is a question that would plague the country for decades to come. At first, the most common explanation was Hölzenbein's alleged dive (a faked foul), which led to an equalizing penalty kick. But this was supplanted by a good dose of self-criticism—for example, by the author Auke Kok, who identified other causes for the failure of Total Soccer in his 2004 book *1974, Wij Waren De Besten (We Were The Best)*: lots of alcohol, little discipline, the arrogance of wanting to beat the West Germans and show them who was who, Cruyff's airs and graces (like his smoking during halftime), and the condescending attitude of coach Michels—he didn't hold a single tactical talk before the final game. ⚽

30 // May

Soccer wins votes. At least this is what some evidence pertaining to the relationship between sports and politics suggest. The probable cause: a country that becomes world champion is more satisfied with itself and with its government than a country that loses. So it's no surprise that a national coach like Helmut Schön, holding the World Cup trophy in his hands, was highly praised by a chancellor like Helmut Schmidt, who was otherwise not terribly interested in the sport.

1978 // Argentina

The high level of freedom that had characterized the game and allowed for exquisite offensive plays in the 1970s was coming slowly to an end. A time of new tactical constraints and defensive systems was approaching. Is it a coincidence that soccer experienced this new lack of freedom in an authoritarian country? No other World Cup has been as controversial as the one in Argentina in 1978. The tournament took place two years after the military coup, and political and economic doubts about the venue abounded. These doubts overshadowed the entire tournament and led to a very tense atmosphere. Indeed, this was a World Cup that most people, except perhaps those in Argentina itself, would rather forget.

XI
Campeonato
Mundial
de Fútbol

Junio 1978

Buenos Aires
Córdoba
Mar del Plata
Mendoza
Rosario

Argentina '78

FIRST ROUND, GROUP A

Italy vs. France 2–1
Argentina vs. Hungary 2–1
Italy vs. Hungary 3–1
Argentina vs. France 2–1
France vs. Hungary 3–1
Italy vs. Argentina 1–0

RESULTS
1. Italy (Points: 6, Goals: 6–2)
2. Argentina (4, 4–3)
3. France (2, 5–5)
4. Hungary (0, 3–8)

FIRST ROUND, GROUP B

Germany vs. Poland 0–0
Tunisia vs. Mexico 3–1
Poland vs. Tunisia 1–0
Germany vs. Mexico 6–0
Poland vs. Mexico 3–1
Germany vs. Tunisia 0–0

RESULTS
1. Poland (Points: 5, Goals: 4–1)
2. Germany (4, 6–0)
3. Tunisia (3, 3–2)
4. Mexico (0, 2–12)

FIRST ROUND, GROUP C

Austria vs. Spain 2–1
Brazil vs. Sweden 1–1
Austria vs. Sweden 1–0
Brazil vs. Spain 0–0
Spain vs. Sweden 1–0
Brazil vs. Austria 1–0

RESULTS
1. Austria (Points: 4, Goals: 3–2)
2. Brazil (4, 2–1)
3. Spain (3, 2–2)

FIRST ROUND, GROUP D

Peru vs. Scotland 3–1
Holland vs. Iran 3–0
Scotland vs. Iran 1–1
Holland vs. Peru 0–0
Peru vs. Iran 4–1
Scotland vs. Holland 3–2

RESULTS
1. Peru (Points: 5, Goals: 7–2)
2. Holland (3, 5–3)
3. Scotland (3, 5–6)

SECOND ROUND, GROUP 1

Italy vs. Germany 0–0
Holland vs. Austria 5–1
Holland vs. Germany 2–2
Italy vs. Austria 1–0
Holland vs. Italy 2–1
Austria vs. Germany 3–2

RESULTS

1. Holland (Points: 5, Goals: 9–4)
2. Italy (3, 2–2)
3. Germany (2, 4–5)
4. Austria (2, 4–8)

SECOND ROUND, GROUP 2

Brazil vs. Peru 3–0
Argentina vs. Poland 2–0
Poland vs. Peru 1–0
Argentina vs. Brazil 0–0
Brazil vs. Poland 3–1
Argentina vs. Peru 6–0

RESULTS

1. Argentina (Points: 5, Goals: 8–0)
2. Brazil (5, 6–1)
3. Poland (2, 2–5)
4. Peru (0, 0–10)

THIRD-PLACE MATCH

Brazil vs. Italy 2–1

FINAL

Argentina vs. Holland 3–1 OT

World Cup Champion: ARGENTINA

2 // June

1978 // Argentina

The geometry of a global game: trying to fit a round ball into a square hole—into the goal, that is. The goal is on the rectangular playing field, which is surrounded by the oval arena; and what happens in this space moves a slightly larger sphere, namely the entire world. From a small ball to the globe, the whole thing comes full circle—just like the extravagant 1978 World Cup opening ceremony in the River Plate Stadium in Buenos Aires.

3 // June

> The general and junta leader Jorge Rafael Videla in civilian clothes at the opening ceremony.
< A military dictatorship exerts its influence over the World Cup: instead of the police, the army monitors the access roads to the stadium in Cordoba.

A civilian setting for a spectacular sporting event: Argentina's ruler Jorge Rafael Videla left his general's uniform in the closet to present a peaceful image at the opening of the World Cup. But the worldwide criticism of a military dictatorship being selected to host the World Cup didn't let up during the tournament.

1978 // Argentina

4 // June

> Musicians in the Rosario Stadium.
< Sports photographers on June 21, 1978, in Rosario Stadium at the Argentina vs. Peru game, which ended 6–0 for the host country.

Soccer as a global reflection, mirrored in the military band's tubas and photographers' lenses: every four years, the world indulges in a confection made according to a classic recipe—goals and wins. A soccer fan's sustenance centers around these two ingredients. ⚽

5 // June

> Hans Müller man-on-man with the Pole Adam Nawalka.

< The Polish goalkeeper Jan Tomaszewski.

The World Cup traditionally is opened by the title-holder. But sometimes it's difficult to recognize the former champions—as was the case with Germany in 1978. Gerd Müller wasn't the only teammate to announce his retirement after having won the world title in 1974. In 1977, the greatest German soccer player of all time said his farewells: Franz Beckenbauer transferred to the U.S. Soccer League to play for the New York Cosmos, pocketing $2.5 million for the switch. In his place, a new face appeared on the scene: twenty-year-old Hans Müller from Stuttgart. But even he couldn't beat Poland's goalkeeper Jan Tomaszewski. The opening game between Germany and Poland ended like all other World Cup openers between 1962 and 1982: with no goals. ⚽

6 // June

England didn't qualify—so Scotland represented the motherland of soccer at the 1978 World Cup. Expectations soared after European champion Czechoslovakia was eliminated in the qualifying round, even if the victor, Scotland, was a bit confused with regard to geography. "We're on the way to Rio!" reported the headline of a Scottish newspaper when it became clear that Scotland would be participating in the World Cup. But in the end, they still made it to the right country, Argentina. And in the first game against Peru, everything started out according to plan: in the 14th minute, Joe Jordan brought his team into the lead with 1–0. But then everything took a turn for the worse. ⚽

7 // June

Teofilo Cubillas was one of the big discoveries of the 1970 World Cup. Eight years later, some people already were dismissing him as too old, even though he was only twenty-nine. But, as it turns out, he became the first star of the 1978 games. He played a brilliant match against Scotland, assisting with the equalizer and scoring two fantastic goals for a 3–1 victory. The Scots, who had been dreaming of the title, didn't recover and failed to deliver in the final round—as has been the case in each of the eight World Cups in which the team has participated so far. With their elegant performance, however, the Peruvians were a real crowd-pleaser and created what was to become a classic look in sports apparel. Even today, their extravagant uniforms with a red diagonal stripe are a must-have in retro fashion.

8 // June

1978 // Argentina

Tu felix Austria—the time when Austria and Spain were joined together to exert their influence on world politics lies centuries in the past, a fact that Spain soon got a whiff of in Argentina. Hans Krankl, the son of a Viennese trolley driver, scored for a final 2–1. Along with goalkeeper Friedrich Koncilia, he laid the foundation for the team's stunning success in that year's World Cup. ⚽

9 // June

Argentina is not the first host nation to have the referees give them the benefit of the doubt. Sometimes a team needs this help to make it through the preliminary round. Like this scene here: Frenchman Marius Trésor tackles Leopoldo Luque, falls, and lands on the ball with his forearm—a textbook case of an unintentional handball that shouldn't be penalized. Yet referee Dubach, in a break with the usual policy of Swiss neutrality, gave the Argentineans a penalty kick, only later to withhold a fully justified one from France. Argentina won 2–1 and avoided an embarrassment that has yet to befall a World Cup host: being eliminated in the first round. ⚽

10 // June

> Reigning world-champion Germany gives a disappointing performance in the 0–0 draw against Tunisia.

< The German goalkeeper Sepp Maier.

Twilight in Córdoba, and twilight of the gods in the 1974 World Cup: goalkeeper Sepp Maier kept a clinically clean sheet in the qualifier. Yet, just like in the game against Poland, Germany didn't do better than a 0–0 draw, forecasting an unsuccessful defense of the title. The tally 0–0, the saddest of all results in soccer, one which stifles the imagination: "A 0–0 stares at me like two gaping, yawning mouths," wrote the soccer poet Eduardo Galeano.

1978 // Argentina

11 // June

The world of this major sporting event remained rather small for quite some time: Europe and South America were practically the only continents on the World Cup map for many decades. The discovery of Africa in the world of soccer wasn't until the 1970s. Tunisia set the stage with its impressive performance, beating the more established Mexicans and wresting a 0–0 from world-champion Germany, only to be eliminated in an unlucky 0–1 loss to Poland. This showed that the so-called Soccer Dwarves were not just fillers and colorful accents for the World Cup: with turbans, kaffiyehs, national flags, and patriotic cheers, the Tunisian fans were truly a valuable addition to the game. ⚽

> Teofilo Cubillas is unstoppable, as Iran's goalkeeper Nasser Hejazi finds out, converting a penalty kick for Peru.

< Peruvian fans in their national colors, red and white, as they defeat Iran 4–1.

The phrase "the goalkeeper's fear of the penalty kick" entered general usage in 1970 with the publication of a story of the same title by the Austrian writer Peter Handke. Eight years later in Peru's 4–1 win over Iran, Teofilo Cubillas showed that at least goalkeeper Nasser Hejazi had a good reason to fear it: in only four minutes, Cubillas converted two penalty kicks.

13 // June

Human walls: there are two moments in which players stand shoulder to shoulder, building an imposing wall. One is when they pose as a team for the cameras and national anthem before the game (photo, right). The other is when they attempt to block the opponent's direct line into the goal during a free kick (photo, left). However, in this case, the heads of the Austrians here looking back to the goal show that these six men let one past.

1978 // Argentina

14 // June

Catenaccio **refers to the most defensive** of all soccer strategies. It was invented by a man from Switzerland, but perfected by the Italians. When an important game hangs in the balance, especially in the World Cup, the *catenaccio* always is pulled out of the hat. This tried-and-true defense strategy gives players a sense of security and can wear down the opponent. It can be a particularly tough test for strikers, as Karl-Heinz Rummenigge found out in his attempt against Antonio Cabrini. For goalkeepers, however, such as Sepp Maier and Dino Zoff (left photo), it can provide a cushion. Germany vs. Italy: the final score was, of course, 0-0. ⚽

15 // June

No other team lost the World title by as narrow a margin as Holland: first in 1974 in the final game in Munich, then again in 1978 with virtually the same lineup they had used in the previous World Cup. Sports can provide the winners with unforgettable memories, but this applies to the losers as well: the quiet tragedy of a moment lost by a fraction of a second, the chance of a lifetime lost by an inch. But nobody has ever gotten as close to victory as Holland's Rob Rensenbrink. In Argentina he became a star, scoring five goals in five games, including the thousandth goal in World Cup history, and leading his team into the final game with a 2–2 draw with Germany. In the championship final, the score was 1–1 in the 90th. He gained possession of the ball, shot left—and hit the left post. Nothing more than a piece of wood had turned Holland's dream of becoming World Champion into an eternal "What if?" ⚽

16 // June

> The German team leader Berti Vogts.

< Innovation in action: Bruno Pezzey (Austria) and Francesco Graziani (Italy) exchange shorts.

A black-and-white armband with the words "team leader"—Berti Vogts wore this status symbol as a *primus inter pares* (first among equals) during the 1978 World Cup, but it didn't bring him or his team any luck. In his last game, he paved the way to a 2–3 defeat to Austria with an own goal. Players aren't quite as attached to other articles of clothing: after the final whistle they exchange their jerseys with those of their opponents without a second thought. But in the intermediate round of the 1978 World Cup, the Austrian Bruno Pezzey and the Italian Francesco Graziani surprised the soccer world with a much more innovative form of clothing exchange: they traded shorts! ⚽

17 // June

> The German Rolf Rüßmann (above) and the Austrian Bruno Pezzey in aerial combat in the Córdoba Stadium.
< Karl-Heinz Rummenigge helps the Austrian Erich Obermeyer to his feet.

The airspace over Córdoba, filled with headers and pulsating voices and cheers—the ingredients for a game that would become part of German-Austrian soccer folklore like no other. A clear victory would have helped Germany make it into the final game. But the 1974 champions were dethroned when they lost to their small neighbor for the first time in forty-seven years and didn't even make it into the game for third place. When Hans Krankl notched the winning goal for a 3–2 final score just before the final whistle, Austrian radio listeners experienced reporter Edi Finger's now-famous burst of emotion. Alongside six "GOOOAAAL" cries and a "VICTORY!" refrain repeated thirteen times, more than any other moment in sports radio history, it is Finger's exclamation, *"I werd narrisch!"* ("I'm going crazy!") that has become permanently engraved in Austrians' collective memory. ⚽

1978 // Argentina

18 // June

> The stellar finisher Ernie Brandts (below) is bowled over by the bubbling cheers of the Dutch team.

< The Dutchman Wim Jansen (left) man-on-man with the Italian Franco Causio.

1978 // Argentina

Some people just can't delegate responsibility. They have to do everything themselves. Ernie Brandts, for example, didn't only take care of the goal for his own team, he also scored for his opponent. After his own goal for Italy, the Dutchman was able to make amends with his equalizer. In the end, Arie Haan scored as well, and Holland pulled into the final game with a 2–1 victory over Italy. ⚽

19 // June

> Closing cheers after the "minifinal": Brazil beats Italy 2–1 and takes third place in the 1978 World Cup.

< Three-time world champion Pelé as a commentator in the final round, Argentina vs. Brazil.

If there were a competition for the best names, Brazil would win the world title for sure. The names in its lineup are always music to the ears. But with Nelinho, Roberto Dinamite, Oscar, Amaral, Gil, Mendonça, Rodrigues Neto, Batista, Leão, Cerezo, and Dirceu on the ball, they were nevertheless stuck in third place. It might have had something to do with the fact that the great Edson Arantes do Nascimento, aka Pelé, didn't appear on the pitch anymore, but at the microphone. ⚽

1978 // Argentina

20 // June

Super Mario: the name of a short plumber with a moustache who first saw the light of day in the world of video games in 1983 and quickly became one of the most famous video game characters worldwide. Yet it was the Argentineans who discovered the first real-life Super Mario five years before the Japanese did. His name: Super Mario Kempes. When he scored, he scored double—in the World Cup final round against Poland and Peru and in the final game against Holland. Here he celebrates the first goal against Peru, a game in which Argentina had to win by four goals in order to pass Brazil and make it into the final. The team won 6–0, and, because the home video recorder had just been invented and people can never see enough goals, Mario Kempes became in 1978 what Super Mario became only later: a video-game star. ⚽

21 // June

Soccer as a game of colors: tens of thousands of excited Argentineans frame the championship final in blue and white. But for their millions of fellow countrymen at home, it remained a colorless event. Though Argentinean television broadcast color images of the World Cup throughout the world, cost considerations meant the World Cup was only in black and white on Argentinean televisions in 1978.

1978 // Argentina

22 // June

The shorts were never as short and the shirts were never as skin-tight as they were in the 1978 World Cup, when a form-fitting style was en vogue in the sport. In particular, the Argentinean Mario Kempes wowed the crowds not only as a superb striker, but also as a male model. He decided the final game with two goals; with a total of six goals, he was the highest-scoring player in the World Cup, which, incidentally, marks the first time in the history of the World Cup that the winning team also boasted the Golden Boot.

23 // June

> Legs up: the Dutch Jan Poortvliet (left) and Wim Suurbier try to protect the ball from Mario Kempes.

< Alberto Tarantini (left) and Daniel Passarella put the brakes on Johan Neeskens.

The Argentinean striker Mario Kempes got past the Dutch defense three times in the final game, scoring the first goal for a 1–0 stand in the first half, the second (2–1) in overtime, and, after a double pass, assisted his teammate Daniel Bertoni, climbing up 3–1. With this, the Argentineans, playing on their native continent, continued a unique trend: South American teams had won all World Cups in the Americas, and European teams all World Cups in Europe. Only one team had been able to break the rule: Brazil, 1958, in Sweden.

24 // June

No, even soccer can't make vegetarians out of a country so famous for its steaks, even though the picture to the right might suggest otherwise. But don't be fooled, this isn't a picture of a health-food nut, but rather a deeply moved fan kissing the victory-christened pitch of River Plate Stadium in Buenos Aires. Argentina's first world title unleashed a collective euphoria, taking thousands in the stadium and millions in the entire country with it.

1978 // Argentina

25 // June

> For anyone who still couldn't believe it after the final game, the scoreboard displays loud and clear: Argentina is the world champion!
< Argentina's team captain Daniel Passarella with the FIFA trophy.

Soccer: a modern-day opiate of the masses. A world title won on native soil bestows a nationwide feeling of joy and unity. Yet this didn't do anything for the military rulers in Buenos Aires. The victory of the national team didn't make the junta more popular—quite the contrary. The Argentinean coach Cesar Luis Menotti would later assert that this World Cup success was the first step in shaking off the tyranny of the ruling regime. Immediately following the World Cup, he expressed these thoughts in diplomatic code. Although he was explicitly referring to the game, his comments obviously had a political undertone: "My talented, smart players conquered the dictatorship of tactics and the terror of the system."

1978 // Argentina

SEIKO
CRONOMETRO OFICIAL
12
PERIODO
ARGENTINA
TIEMPO DE JUEGO
¡CAMPEON!
STEWART - WARNER
AUTOTROL

1982 // Spain

- 26 // June
> 27 // June

Soccer as a fine art: as the thirteenth host of the World Cup, Spain illustrated this thought nicely—the country hired the artist Joan Miró to design the official poster. But there were other great artists involved in the World Cup as well: the players on the field. When it came to their artistry in front of the goal, however, they had a harder time of it than their counterparts at the easel, who didn't have to worry about fouls or persistent defenders. Brazil had the most fantastic team and Argentina had the most graceful players in the world, yet both were beaten by the tough Italians. France wowed spectators with its offense, but was defeated by the colorless Germans. The 1982 World Cup also marked a new understanding of soccer—not as a fine art, but rather as an art of survival. And it is this art that has produced the world champion ever since.

FIRST ROUND, GROUP A

Italy vs. Poland 0–0
Peru vs. Cameroon 0–0
Italy vs. Peru 1–1
Poland vs. Cameroon 0–0
Poland vs. Peru 5–1
Italy vs. Cameroon 1–1

RESULTS
1. Poland (Points: 4, Goals: 5–1)
2. Italy (3, 2–2)
3. Cameroon (3, 1–1)
4. Peru (2, 2–6)

FIRST ROUND, GROUP B

Algeria vs. Germany 2–1
Austria vs. Chile 1–0
Germany vs. Chile. 4–1
Austria vs. Algeria 2–0
Algeria vs. Chile 3–2
Germany vs. Austria 1–0

RESULTS
1. Germany (Points: 4, Goals: 6–3)
2. Austria (4, 3–1)
3. Algeria (4, 5–5)
4. Chile (0, 3–8)

FIRST ROUND, GROUP C

Belgium vs. Argentina 1–0
Hungary vs. El Salvador 10–1
Argentina vs. Hungary 4–1
Belgium vs. El Salvador 1–0
Belgium vs. Hungary 1–1
Argentina vs. El Salvador 2–0

RESULTS
1. Belgium (Points: 5, Goals: 3–1)
2. Argentina (4, 6–2)
3. Hungary (3, 12–6)
4. El Salvador (0, 1–13)

FIRST ROUND, GROUP D

England vs. France 3–1
Czechoslovakia vs. Kuwait 1–1
England vs. Czechoslovakia 2–0
France vs. Kuwait 4–1
France vs. Czechoslovakia 1–1
England vs. Kuwait 1–0

RESULTS
1. England (Points: 6, Goals: 6–1)
2. France (3, 6–5)
3. Czechoslovakia (2, 2–4)
4. Kuwait (1, 2–6)

FIRST ROUND, GROUP E

Spain vs. Honduras 1–1
Yugoslavia vs. Northern Ireland 0–0
Spain vs. Yugoslavia 2–1
Honduras vs. Northern Ireland 1–1
Yugoslavia vs. Honduras 1–0
Northern Ireland vs. Spain 1–0

RESULTS
1. Northern Ireland (Points: 4, Goals: 2–1)
2. Spain (3, 3–3)
3. Yugoslavia (3, 2–2)
4. Honduras (2, 2–3)

FIRST ROUND, GROUP F

Brazil vs. Soviet Union 2–1
Scotland vs. New Zealand 5–2
Brazil vs. Scotland 4–1
Soviet Union vs. New Zealand 3–0
Soviet Union vs. Scotland 2–2
Brazil vs. New Zealand 4–0

RESULTS
1. Brazil (Points: 6, 10–2)
2. Soviet Union (3, 6–4)
3. Scotland (3, 8–8)
4. New Zealand (0, 2–12)

SECOND ROUND, GROUP 1

Poland vs. Belgium 3–0
Belgium vs. Soviet Union 0–1
Poland vs. Soviet Union 0–0

RESULTS

1. Poland (Points: 3, Goals: 3–0)
2. Soviet Union (3, 1–0)
3. Belgium (0, 0–4)

SECOND ROUND, GROUP 2

Germany vs. England 0–0
Germany vs. Spain 2–1
Spain vs. England 0–0

RESULTS

1. Germany (Points: 3, Goals: 2–1)
2. England (2, 0–0)
3. Spain (1, 1–2)

SECOND ROUND, GROUP 3

Italy vs. Argentina 2–1
Brazil vs. Argentina 3–1
Italy vs. Brazil 3–2

RESULTS

1. Italy (Points: 4, Goals: 5–3)
2. Brazil (2, 5–4)
3. Argentina (0, 2–5)

SECOND ROUND, GROUP 4

France vs. Austria 1–0
Austria vs. Northern Ireland 2–2
France vs. Northern Ireland 4–1

RESULTS

1. France (Points: 4–0, Goals: 5–1)
2. Austria (1, 2–3)
3. Northern Ireland (1, 3–6)

SEMIFINALS

Italy vs. Poland 2–0
Germany vs. France 8–7 PEN

THIRD-PLACE MATCH

Poland vs. France 3–2

FINAL

Italy vs. Germany 3–1

World Cup Champion: ITALY

28 // June

1982 // Spain

Soccer shows its colors—and there are even more of them this time around. The history of the World Cup began in 1930 with only thirteen participating nations instead of the expected sixteen, because most of the Europeans opted to forgo the long journey by ship to Uruguay. Between 1934 and 1978, the tournament took place with the manageable number of sixteen countries. At the opening ceremony in the Estadio Nou Camp in Barcelona, the national flags of twenty-four participating countries were presented for the first time. But the expansion of the global game wasn't over yet: ever since 1998, a total of thirty-two teams have competed in each World Cup. ⚽

> A defensive fight with the gloves off: no rest for a weary twenty-one-year-old Diego Maradona at his first World Cup.

< Legendary number 10 on Argentina's team has possession.

Morals and morale—are the two words related when it comes to soccer? When a team refuses to let things get it down, people say, "They have good morale!" But what about fair play? Does morale have anything to do with moral or ethical considerations in sports? In everyday life, "morale" and "morals" may have more in common than just five letters. But in soccer, at least, the similarity seems to end there. Indeed, morale in soccer actually can mean trampling on the codes of good sportsmanship. At least this is what one of the most brilliant players of his time, Diego Maradona, found out in the game against Italy: defender Claudio Gentile was entrusted with the sole task of stopping the twenty-one-year-old star by any means possible, many of which were against the rules. But it worked. Italy won, and titleholder Argentina found itself in the same situation as Maradona after having been fouled a dozen times: wiped out.

30 // June

The old man and the goal: Dino Zoff could follow the ball in the qualifier against Peru with complete composure. Even at the age of forty, the Italian goalkeeper exuded calmness and a feline elegance that he had learned in the old school. In 1982, he became the oldest world champion in soccer history. ⚽

1982 // Spain

1 // July

The joy of the beautiful male physique: soccer is played mostly with the lower body, but the upper body can stand to be seen every once in while. In 1982, spectators had to wait until the final whistle to be able to steal a peek at partially unclothed players (like these four Peruvians). A good ten years later, much to the joy of female fans, in a new trend for celebrating goals, players would tear their jerseys off—a popular striptease that could only be put in check when the lawmakers of the game decided to make the spectacle punishable by a yellow card. ⚽

2 // July

Africa's colors enriched the 1982 World Cup—yet the continent, first represented with two countries, didn't reap any reward for its contribution. In this photograph, Algeria's goalkeeper Mahdi Cerbah celebrates his team's sensational 2–1 victory over Germany with one of his fans—but the North Africans disappointed in the qualifying round, thanks to Austria and Germany's tricks in the scandalous Gijon game. Buoyed by its colorful fans, Cameroon remained undefeated in three games, only to suffer a defeat in the qualifying round—even though the team had the same number of goals and the same goal differential as soon-to-be-world-champion Italy. Africa brought joy to the game, but it was the joyless game of the Europeans that ultimately led to success. ⚽

1982 // Spain

3 **// July**

1982 // Spain

A soccer decathlon, first event: the dash for the ball turned the Pole Stefan Majewski and the Cameroonian Jacques N'guea into sprinters. The winner of the race (and, of course, the ball) is unknown—all we know is that he wasn't able to do much with his minor victory: the game ended 0–0. ⚽

4 // July

Arabian influence in Spain—reawakened five hundred years after the Moors—was one of Kuwait's contributions to the World Cup. Accompanied by the music of the shalm and the applause of fans sporting a variety of head scarves, the World Cup newcomers wrestle a 1–1 draw out of the Czechoslovakian favorites. ⚽

5 // July

Every fan's dream: to rush out onto the field when his team has been treated unfairly and make everything better. Believe it or not, this actually happened in the 4–1 game between France and Kuwait in 1982, making for a one-of-a-kind scene in the history of soccer. The Frenchman Alain Giresse scored, and the Soviet referee Stupar called the goal. Furious, the president of the Kuwaiti Football Association, Prince Fahd Al-Ahmad, forced his way onto the field along with one of his wives. Utter chaos broke out. The referee tried in vain to give orders, and the police marched in. And what did the referee do? At the behest of the prince, he rescinded the goal. ⚽

6 // July

1982 // Spain

When it comes to hairstyles, at least, it's not really necessary for players to be on the ball. The Frenchman Michel Platini's head of black frizz and the glorious blond curls of the Austrian, Herbert Prohaska—both of them great midfield strategists—were still in line with the trends of the time. After all, in 1982 it was stylish to wear a mane of curls, whether they were bestowed by nature or created with the help of a perm.

7 // July

So close, but yet so far: a young fan watches his stars through the fence (photo right), and a young player watches his teammates from the sidelines. It's Lothar Matthäus, who is waiting here for his chance to play in what will be the first of many World Cups over the course of his long career. His substitution in the 4–1 victory over Chile was the first of a total of twenty-five World Cup games—a record that places the German player a cut above all the rest.

1982 // Spain

8 // July

> A friendly chat in the infamous game nicknamed the Nonaggression Pact of Gijon: Karl-Heinz Rummenigge (Germany) and Bruno Pezzey (Austria, right).

Competitive sports can be this easy: languid soccer with Pezzey, Rummenigge, and, in the background, Felix Magath—who at least is moving! With Hrubesch's goal for a 1–0 lead for Germany in the qualifier against Austria, both teams automatically qualified for the next round, at the expense of the powerless Algerians. As a result, 1–0 was the final score—after eighty minutes of the players doing nothing. This most embarrassing of all soccer matches, the so-called Nonaggression Pact of Gijon, offended the world and hurt the German team's reputation more than any defeat could have.

9 // July

Algerian fans waved bills around to show what they thought of the game between Germany and Austria: this was soccer betrayed and sold. The Spanish newspaper *As* wrote of the "burglary of the century." "The only thing missing was that they didn't kiss," complained *El País*. The French coach Michel Hidalgo ironically nominated both teams for the Nobel peace prize. And the paper *El Comercio* decided to print the write-up on the game not in the sports section, but in the police blotter. ⚽

1982 // Spain

10 // July

The sheer allure of men's legs—no fashion really does them justice. Bermuda shorts, kilts, or leggings, nothing seems to measure up aesthetically to hairy male limbs. Nothing, that is, except for soccer shorts. Short, loose, baggy to the knee, or wide-legged, every four years the world looks to men's legs for a change of pace. Yet only one pair of soccer legs has made it onto the hit parade: they belonged to Karl-Heinz Rummenigge. The pop duo Alan & Denise wrote a song about him: "Over in West Germany there's a man with sexy knees . . . Rummenigge, all night long . . . two legs long but all beyond." ⚽

1982 // Spain

11 // July

> Bruno Pezzey (right) tries to keep William Hamilton out of the game.

< Austrians Bruno Pezzey (left) and Reinhold Hintermaier (right) crowd out the Northern Irishman Martin O'Neill.

Players on their mark have to be social creatures. Their job demands that they build a particularly close relationship with other people—or at least with one person. Sometimes they develop a closeness that can make strikers on the spacious playing field feel like they're stuck in an overcrowded Tokyo subway car. At least this is how William Hamilton must have felt with Bruno Pezzey marking him. But Pezzey's strategy didn't work out quite as he had planned: in the 2–2 draw against Austria in the intermediate round, the Northern Irishman Hamilton scored both goals for his team. ⚽

1982 // Spain

12 // July

> Host Spain in the capital city's stadium:
Santiago Urquiaga wins a 50–50 ball out from
under Pierre Littbarski's nose.

< But in the end, his team loses to Germany 1–2.

Hosting a World Cup is a good way to win it. The home-team advantage can be seen in the statistics: out of the 17 World Cups held between 1930 and 2002, the host team won the title six times, and the home team never once disappointed in the first round. In 1982, Spain followed this example as well—but only by the skin of its teeth. Following a 1–1 draw against Honduras and a 0–1 victory over Northern Ireland, the team was only just able to move on to the next round. In the final round, Spain reached its last stop in the 0–0 draw against England in Madrid's Bernabéu Stadium. In the same stadium, but in another game, Germany won with goals by Pierre Littbarski and Klaus Fischer, conceding one goal to Zamora for a score of 2–1, thus pulling into the semifinal. ⚽

13 // July

> These two were among the best players of their generation: the Englishman Kevin Keegan (left) and the Brazilian Zico.

< Just missed it: the English team plays to a 0-0 draw in the final round against Spain, and Germany makes it into the semifinal.

Unfinished works: Kevin Keegan and Zico are prime examples of divinely gifted players who just happened not to have the luck or the right teammates to make it to the top of a World Cup. Due to a back injury, "Mighty Mouse" Keegan had to wait until the last game to play, and England didn't pull off the win against Spain necessary to make it into the semifinal. Zico, "the White Pelé," shined as always, yet due to notorious weaknesses in defense, his magical Brazilian team lost to Italy with a score of 2–3.

14 // July

1982 // Spain

The last thing that Patrick Battiston saw in this game was this picture, after which he was knocked unconscious. The route that he took from the halfway line to the German goal brought him directly to the hospital. Playing a deep ball, he collided into goalkeeper Harald Schumacher in the 60th minute. Schumacher jumped with his hips and thighs forward, and in a head-on collision crashed into the Frenchman's throat and head, breaking a cervical vertebra and knocking out numerous teeth. For many, this was the most brutal foul in World Cup history. While the horrified French took care of an unconscious Battiston, Schumacher stood by looking bored. The referee granted a penalty kick.

15 // July

True to his name, the Frenchman Trésor (treasure) was an invaluable asset to France's lineup. His stellar defensive game glistened like gold in Spain in 1982, but this wasn't the end of it. During overtime in the dramatic semifinal, the defender pulled his team into the lead. Teammate Alain Giresse brought the score up to 3–1, but then the Germans unlocked their own buried treasure: Rummenigge and Fischer were able to equalize.

1982 // Spain

16 // July

> Germany's specialist in bicycle kicks: Klaus Fischer scores the critical equalizer in the semifinal against France.
< Pierre Littbarski (Germany, left) and Manuel Amoros (France) in a discussion with the Dutch referee, Charles Corver.

The bicycle kick is named after the alternating bicyclelike movement of the swinging and shooting leg—yet this definition hardly does justice to one of the most spectacular ways to shoot a goal. The bicycle kick is said to have been invented by Ramon Unzaga on the soccer field in the Chilean port of Talcahuano. His compatriot David Arellano presented this work of art in Europe for the first time in 1927, when the top Chilean club Colo-Colo had a game in Spain. The most stunning German bicycle trick was to be seen half a century later when Klaus Fischer pulled it to equalize 3–3 against France in overtime in the 1982 World Cup semifinal.

1982 // Spain

17 // July

> Beside themselves: Didier Six (France, left) and Uli Stielike (Germany) after both players miss penalty kicks.

< Pierre Littbarski tries to concentrate before his penalty kick.

The goalkeeper's fear of the penalty kick is nothing compared to that of the shooter. Barely one-tenth of all penalty kicks during normal playing time in the World Cup fail to land in the net. But the number rises to one-fourth when the score is equal after 120 minutes (90 minutes plus 30 minutes of overtime) for the final showdown. In the semifinal in Sevilla, the German Uli Stielike sulked away after an unsuccessful test of his nerves. Later, the Frenchman Didier Six buried his face in his hands: no goal. In the end, his compatriot Bossis missed as well, and Germany was in the final game. The French Bleus had the penalty-kick blues. ⚽

18 // July

The game for third place is an unloved event. Those who play in it would rather be in the final game—or on their way home. But they have to stay. Often, replacements are played, and usually it's the team that doesn't lament the missed chance to play in the final that wins—the mere fact that the players reached the semifinal already exceeds all of their expectations. This wasn't the case with France. Its players couldn't come to terms with their defeat to Germany. The Polish team saw its chance and went on to win 3–2.

1982 // Spain

19 // July

> The Italian team before the opening whistle of the final game in Madrid's Estadio Santiago Bernabéu.

< Team portrait of the other participant in the final game, Germany.

White giants: the Italian team presents itself pure as spring blossoms in all their innocence for the final game—and this only a few years after the Toto Nero betting scandal in Italian professional soccer. Dozens of corrupt top players had been involved, including the striker Paolo Rossi (fourth from the right). Due to a two-year expulsion, he had been prohibited from playing in the World Cup. But coach Enzo Bearzot successfully lobbied for an amnesty for the top striker, who went on to become top scorer in the World Cup, scoring three goals against Brazil, two against Poland in the semifinal, and the goal that brought his team into the lead against Germany in the final game. ⚽

20 // July

> 1–0 for Italy: Antonio Cabrini breaks away cheering, while striker Paolo Rossi (below) is still tangled up with goalkeeper Toni Schumacher.

< Italy's striker Paolo Rossi.

A goal—it unties every tangled knot of players instantly. The ball is in the net, giving Italy a 1–0 score in the final game. The Italian offense is bursting with energy. The German defenders in the goal look like they've been turned to stone. Never before had Germany seemed so lifeless as in this, the weakest of its seven performances in the World Cup. ⚽

1982 // Spain

21 // July

In 1934, Mussolini simply ordered the Italian team to win the title in its homeland, and carried out his plan with the help of willing referees—as if Nero were still in charge in Rome and deciding who would win various sporting events. In 1938, the title was successfully defended, much to the satisfaction of the fascist dictator. The third Italian World Cup victory didn't have to please any dictator, just the top azzurro, the elderly Italian President Sandro Pertini. In front of him, the German Chancellor Helmut Schmidt, and a worldwide audience of billions, Gaetano Scirea holds high the golden treasure around which the soccer world revolves for four weeks every four years: the World Cup trophy. ⚽

1986 // Mexico

After only sixteen years, the World Cup returned to the blazing heat of Mexico. Colombia initially had won the bid to host the games, but had to back down because of an economic crisis. Mexico took its place and became the first country to host a World Cup twice. When Columbia applied, sixteen countries were to take part, but the number later rose to twenty-four. Increasingly, the competition was becoming a prestigious global event, reflecting the host nation's logistical abilities and presenting a challenge that would take many countries to their limits. Mexico

1986, more than any previous event, became the stage for one player in particular: Diego Armando Maradona, who was at the height of his abilities. His fraudulent goal against England, propelled by the Hand of God and, three minutes later, that most divine of all World Cup goals: whatever Maradona did, it was sure-handed and sure-footed. None of Argentina's European opponents—be it the English, the Belgians, or the Germans in the final—could stop this diminutive player, who almost single-handedly made his country world champion. Nearly all players with offensive panache—the Danes, Soviets, Brazilians, and French—were stymied. All, that is, except Maradona. One could apply the words once coined by Alfred Polgar to describe Matthias Sindelar, the star of the 1930s Austrian Wonder Team: "He had, as it were, character in his legs. As they charged, they would spontaneously come up with a lot of surprising moves."

// The Games

FIRST ROUND, GROUP A

Italy vs. Bulgaria 1–1
Argentina vs. South Korea 3–1
Italy vs. Argentina 1–1
South Korea vs. Bulgaria 1–1
Italy vs. South Korea 3–2
Argentina vs. Bulgaria 2–0

RESULTS
1. Argentina (Points: 5, Goals: 6–2)
2. Italy (4, 5–4)
3. Bulgaria (2, 2–4)
4. South Korea (1, 4–7)

FIRST ROUND, GROUP B

Mexico vs. Belgium 2–1
Paraguay vs. Iraq 1–0
Mexico vs. Paraguay 1–1
Belgium vs. Iraq 2–1
Mexico vs. Iraq 1–0
Belgium vs. Paraguay 2–2

RESULTS
1. Mexico (Points: 5, Goals: 4–2)
2. Paraguay (4, 4–3)
3. Belgium (3, 5–5)
4. Iraq (0, 1–4)

FIRST ROUND, GROUP C

France vs. Canada 1–0
Soviet Union vs. Hungary 6–0
France vs. Soviet Union 1–1
Hungary vs. Canada 2–0
France vs. Hungary 3–0
Soviet Union vs. Canada 2–0

RESULTS
1. Soviet Union (Points: 5, Goals: 9–1)
2. France (5, 5–1)
3. Hungary (2, 2–9)
4. Canada (0, 0–5)

FIRST ROUND, GROUP D

Brazil vs. Spain 1–0
Algeria vs. Northern Ireland 1–1
Brazil vs. Algeria 1–0
Spain vs. Northern Ireland 2–1
Brazil vs. Northern Ireland 3–0
Spain vs. Algeria 3–0

RESULTS
1. Brazil (Points: 6, Goals: 5–0)
2. Spain (4, 5–2)
3. Northern Ireland (1, 2–6)
4. Algeria (1, 1–5)

FIRST ROUND, GROUP E

Germany vs. Uruguay 1–1
Denmark vs. Scotland 1–0
Germany vs. Scotland 2–1
Denmark vs. Uruguay 6–1
Denmark vs. Germany 2–0
Scotland vs. Uruguay 0–0

RESULTS
1. Denmark (Points: 6, Goals: 9–1)
2. Germany (3, 3–4)
3. Uruguay (2, 2–7)
4. Scotland (1, 1–3)

FIRST ROUND, GROUP F

Morocco vs. Poland 0–0
Portugal vs. England 1–0
England vs. Morocco 0–0
Poland vs. Portugal 1–0
Morocco vs. Portugal 3–1
England vs. Poland 3–0

RESULTS
1. Morocco (Points: 4, Goals: 3–1)
2. England (3, 3–1)
3. Poland (3, 1–3)
4. Portugal (2, 2–4)

ROUND OF SIXTEEN

Mexico vs. Bulgaria 2–0
Belgium vs. Soviet Union 4–3 OT
Brazil vs. Poland 4–0
Argentina vs. Uruguay 1–0
France vs. Italy 2–0
Germany vs. Morocco 1–0
England vs. Paraguay 3–0
Spain vs. Denmark 5–1

QUARTERFINALS

France vs. Brazil 5–4 PEN
Germany vs. Mexico 4–1 PEN
Argentina vs. England 2–1
Belgium vs. Spain 6–5 PEN

SEMIFINALS

Germany vs. France 2–0
Argentina vs. Belgium 2–0

THIRD-PLACE MATCH

France vs. Belgium 4–2 OT

FINAL

Argentina vs. Germany 3–2

World Cup Champion: ARGENTINA

An Aztec kicking a ball: perhaps not as far-fetched as it sounds. Nowadays, with the world revolving around an industrial product made up of twenty hexagons and twelve pentagons of synthetic material, it's easy to forget that people have always displayed astounding inventiveness when it has come to ball games. Eskimos used sealskin balls filled with dried moss or bundles of fur. The ancient Chinese kicked leather sacks stuffed with feathers. In Hawaii, the ball was called a popo and was made of leaf wrappings and rags. The Australian aborigines stuffed grass into a kangaroo's scrotum. On the Fiji Islands they played with grapefruits. And a couple of thousand years before the World Cup in Mexico, the locals enjoyed their own brand of soccer: the Aztecs kicked balls made of raw rubber.

> Shade-gear that also guarantees plenty of sitting room all around: the sombrero is the ideal item for matches in the midday sun.
< World Cup fashion à la Mexico: the sombrero and the tuxedo.

Soccer and sombrero: a good idea. Because the European television channels used their clout to secure evening transmission schedules for their viewers, most of the 1986 matches were held in the blazing heat of the Mexican midday. The players protested, most of all Diego Maradona, but to no avail. They had to brave the grueling heat without hats, obviously. At least the fans had their sombreros. ⚽

26 // July

Gaetano Scirea controlled the ball and the game with the elegance of the classic sweeper—a majestic, rather static position, largely redundant since the highly mobile three- and four-man backfield defense strategies emerged in the 1990s. In 1982 he was world champion with Italy, and in 1986 he captained a much weaker *squadra azzura* during the opening match against Bulgaria, ending in a 1–1 draw. Three years later Scirea was killed in a car accident.

1986 // Mexico

> Jean-Pierre Papin (right), who scored the 1–0 winning goal for France in the initial round against Canada.
< Michel Platini, captain of the French national team.

. . . .

. . . .

. . . .

. . . .

When a name means fame: Jean-Pierre Papin shot such spectacular goals during his career that he gave birth to a new term. When someone scores from a difficult, almost impossible, position, French soccer aficionados describe this as a *papinade*. A similar honor was once bestowed upon Germany's top scorer Gerd Müller. He's the role model for goals that deserve the term *müllern*—ones that aren't necessarily spectacular, but result from intuition. ⚽

28 // July

1986 // Mexico

Man-to-man marking for Maradona: when it came to stopping the world's best player, most opponents resorted to an ancient formula, as did the Koreans. But they paid a high price during their 1–3 defeat: two fouls against Maradona, two penalties—and two goals for Argentina.

29 // July

> **Preliminary round, Mexico vs. Belgium (2–1):**
Hugo Sanchez in goal euphoria.
< **Hugo Sanchez apologizing after a foul.**

The athlete among the scorers: Hugo Sanchez modestly celebrating his 2–0 goal against Bulgaria, presumably to save his strength for the second-half showdown in the glaring heat of Mexico City's Aztec Stadium. Normally, the Mexican striker would perform his trademark victory somersault, as later performed by talented colleagues like Germany's Miroslav Klose and the Republic of Ireland's Robbie Keane. The Nigerian player Julius Aghahowa went further still and sometimes managed nearly a dozen of them.

30 // July

Anticipation is better than the event itself: unfortunately this is true of many soccer games. One hundred fifteen thousand spectators in the Aztec Stadium were thrilled at the prospect of seeing Mexico pitted against Paraguay, but the actual match consisted of more pauses than highlights. They witnessed fifty-five fouls, five yellow cards, seventy-eight free kicks (forty-six for Mexico; thirty-two for Paraguay) and only two goals (final score: 1–1). Bodily attacks weren't punished as rigorously as they would be in the 1990s and thereafter. As a result, heel- and rib-bashing were trademarks of this World Cup. This was particularly true of the team from Uruguay, which set a world championship record with a disqualification after only 55 seconds: Batista during the match against Scotland, for a foul so ferocious he received a reprimand from FIFA.

1986 // Mexico

> Pierre Littbarski (right) outsmarts Maurice
Malpas in the Germany-Scotland (2–1) qualifier.
< The German and the Scottish teams walk
onto the playing field.

1986 // Mexico

What's the appeal of soccer? It's often not a man's naked legs, like these bow-legged specimens displayed by German Pierre Littbarski while tackling the Scottish player Malpas. Soccer players don't exhibit muscular elegance, like the erotic thigh jut of the high jumper, the voluminous biceps of the prize-fighter, or the broad shoulders of the butterfly swimmer. Soccer players have arched, flat, or splayed feet, bandy or knocked legs (or all of these at once); they have crooked toes and sore knees—ailments deriving from their brutal sport, not to mention thinning hair due to too many headers. In these cases there must be other factors that make soccer appealing. ⚽

An immortal spectacle, the lanky, elegant Brazilian game master: Sócrates Brasileiro Sampaio de Souza Vieira de Oliveira, son of an Amazonian tax official and self-taught philosopher who gave three of his six sons names from Plato's *Republic* (Socrates, Sostenes, and Sophocles). Sócrates was a soccer wizard, medical doctor, socialist, chain-smoker, father of five sons, and a team captain who brandished political slogans on his headband. In 1982 and 1986, Sócrates starred in Brazilian World Cup teams that failed with brilliant soccer: a romantic era in which "we used the ball to express our emotions," as Sócrates put it. After leaving the sport, he became a medical practitioner, fought against corruption in the Brazilian soccer world and, at the age of 50, made a brief comeback with the English nonleague club Garforth. ⚽

2 // August

> Euphoric Danish fans celebrate their team's 2–0 victory over Germany.

< Danish captain Morten Olsen complains to the referee after Frank Arnesen (on the ground) is sent off.

Danish Dynamite, a new trademark: thousands of fans clad in red and white celebrated defeating Germany 2–0, the team's third victory in as many games at Denmark's first-ever World Cup. The small country, which didn't even feature on the professional world soccer map until the 1970s, conquered the hearts of millions of neutral soccer enthusiasts during the 1986 World Cup, when it beat Uruguay 6–1. It hardly made a difference that the players' fresh, though somewhat naïve, tactics got them badly mauled by Spain in the round of sixteen. The Danish Dynamite delivered a real blast six years later, when they were recalled from vacation to replace Yugoslavia, going on to win in a sensational European Championship.

3 // August

The end of an era: with his 4–3 goal in overtime, Belgian Nico Claesen robbed the Soviet Union of its final chance to conquer the soccer world as a communist state. The Eastern bloc was never that lucky when it came to world-championship soccer. When it did produce a great team, it was always from one of the dissident states at its outer edges, like Hungary in the 1950s, Czechoslovakia in the 1960s, or Poland in the 1970s. Each of them fell just short of victory, their populaces following their team's example a few years later in attempting to liberate themselves from Moscow's domination, as if the playing field were a dress rehearsal for freedom. This even applied to the Soviet Union itself: during the period of perestroika, the players seemed unleashed, putting in amazing performances during the 1986 World Cup qualifying round—until they were eliminated by the Belgians in the round of sixteen. ⚽

4 // **August**

Soccer, a game for mobile people and their offspring: Yannick Stopyra was a Frenchman with a Polish grandfather, his opponent Pietro Vierchowod an Italian of Russian descent. The defending World Cup champion's defeat in the round of sixteen was in large part delivered by French idol Michel Platini, born in the German province of Lorraine, the grandson of an Italian. ⚽

5 // August

His hand was bruised, but Gary Lineker could rely on his head and his feet: the English striker's hat trick against Poland in the qualifier was followed by two goals during the confrontation with Paraguay 3–0 in the round of sixteen. In the following game against Argentina, he only scored a late equalizer after two goals from Maradona. But with six goals in total he became the leading scorer in 1986—no other player of a team that was defeated before reaching the semifinal ever managed this. ⚽

6 // August

Netting it: ball and opponent. Andoni Goicoechea doesn't give goalkeeper Lars Høgh a chance from twelve yards out. It's the third hit for Spain, the 3–1 crusher for the Danes, whose attacks had seemed unstoppable before this game. The final score is 5–1 for Spain. Clearly, the Danes had been lulled into a false sense of security. ⚽

7 // August

> Joint venture: Julio César (Brazil, left) and Jean Tigana (France) chasing the ball.
< Antonio Careca (left) and Manuel Amoros during the quarterfinals, Brazil vs. France (4–5 following penalty shootout).

The three-legged race was a curious event in the infant days of track-and-field. Two sprinters, standing side by side, had their legs tied together, the idea being to somehow coordinate forward movement with a handicap not intended by nature: a runner with three legs. Julio César and Jean Tigana appear to mimic this discipline, perfectly choreographed it would seem, during the World Cup quarterfinal between Brazil and France, joined not by a band, but the competitive urge to get to the ball. ⚽

8 // **August**

> Only milliseconds before Brazil is eliminated: Julio César prepares to take the penalty. It's not French goalkeeper Joël Bats who stops the ball, but the post.

< Zico, the White Pelé, already flunked a penalty-kick test during normal playing time.

Brazil vs. France, a showcase for triumph and tragedy when soccer is played so beautifully—a spectacular performance by both teams, over two hours in the sweltering heat of Guadalajara and perhaps the best game of the decade. The brilliance was enhanced by the fact that the essence of the game—scoring goals—took second place to the sheer enjoyment of playing soccer. Only Careca and Platini scored goals. Both teams had the chance to clinch the game on dozens of occasions. Zico, the White Pelé, even botched a penalty shot. Then, almost like a rude interruption: penalty kicking. And two masters of the art, Sócrates and Platini, fail. Then Julio César hits the post. Brazil loses. "And," as the *Süddeutsche Zeitung* commented, "the samba died a terrible death." ⚽

9 // **August**

> Denmark's defense captain, Morten Olsen
(left), tackling Spanish player Julio Salinas.
< Emilio Butragueño, also called the Vulture.

The Vulture's game: Emilio Butragueño (photo left) was given his nickname because his family name sounded like the name of the bird: *el butro*. In no other game did he do honor to his title as thoroughly as in the World Cup clash with Denmark in the round of sixteen. He equalized shortly before halftime. At this point, the Danes, with their defensive mastermind Morten Olsen, must have sensed what was about to happen—as you do when you see vultures hovering overhead. In the second half Butragueño scored another three goals. ⚽

1986 // Mexico

10 // August

1986 // Mexico

Bilateral cooperation on the soccer field: the German goalkeeper Toni Schumacher displayed fair play by helping Mexican striker Hugo Sanchez, who developed a cramp in his calf during overtime. But the Mexican performance was cramped, too, in the ensuing penalty round—one of three penalty clinchers during the quarterfinals. Schumacher took two penalty shots, Germany won 4–1, and the World Cup host was beaten.

11 // August

> Diego Maradona scores, giving Argentina a
1–0 lead over England, thanks to the Hand of God.
< Helpless in the face of the Hand of God:
England's goalkeeper Peter Shilton (right).

The Hand of God: the term used by Maradona to gain forgiveness for the most controversial goal of his career. "It was the hand of God and the head of Maradona" was his beautifully cryptic comment following the handball incident against England, unfairly slipping the ball past goalkeeper Peter Shilton and the eyes of the Tunisian referee Ali Bennaceur. Maradona's fans sang his praises, true to the popular motto: it's only bad if you get caught. He, on the other hand, who tries to cheat and is caught—like Chile's goalkeeper Roberto Rojas, who, during a World Cup qualifying match in 1990, feigned an injury supposedly caused by fireworks thrown from the crowd—is abandoned by the fans. "Everything I know about morality, I got from playing soccer," wrote Albert Camus, the former Algerian college team goalkeeper and subsequent Nobel laureate for literature. ⚽

12 // August

> Maradona's solo: after his historic sprint across half the pitch, he scores for a 2–0 lead against England.

< Hangover from the Falklands War, which took place only four years prior to the games: a fight between English and Argentinean fans.

The Foot of God: if such a heavenly metaphor were ever permissible within the realms of earthly soccer, then it would apply to Maradona's left foot. Only three minutes after his scandalous handball, the little guy from Argentina managed a feat that was unique in the history of World Cup soccer: going solo from his own half of the field until he got a clear shot at the English goal. It was the goal that gave Argentina its 2–0 lead in the quarterfinal and the decisive move that was to take Argentina toward the final—England only managed to score once, shortly before the game-ending whistle. Much later the English, as so often, would exhibit their sense of fair play: although they were the victims of Maradona's unfair handball, they honored his second strike as Goal of the Century.

13 // August

> Genius Maradona kicking his Goal of the Century—even sixteen years later, during the 2002 World Cup, the fans evoked this event to motivate the Argentinean players.

El gol del siglo—the goal of the century. Sixteen years on (and in an attempt to invoke the sparkle that was missing in the 2002 team) an Argentinean fan displays an image of Maradona's incredible solo performance. The statistics: fifty-four yards from his own half to the opponent's goal area, seven players tackled, including the goalkeeper, eleven ball contacts, all with the left foot, all on the right side of pitch. A goal for the history books.

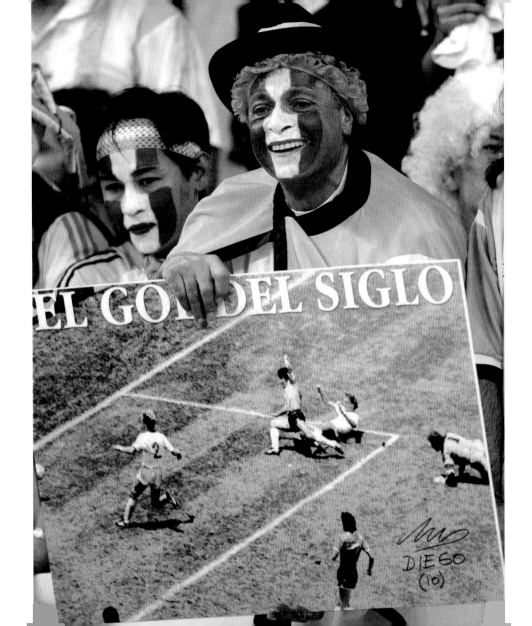

14 // August

When Uruguay first presented South American-style soccer at the 1924 Olympics in Paris—tricks, dribbling, one-two passes—people sought an explanation. A nation of less than two million—purveyors of the world's finest soccer? How was this possible? The star of the team, José Leandro Andrade, gave a rather surprising answer: the interweaving dribble forays were the result of studying hens on the run. Sixty-two years later, during the World Cup quarterfinals, the same technique was witnessed again: a Mexican steward chased a stray rooster through the Aztec Stadium as unsuccessfully as English defenders chased Maradona. Perhaps it also had something to do with the superstitious beliefs of Argentinean coach Carlos Bilardo: He forbade his players to eat chicken, thinking it would bring bad luck. They ate beef instead, and became world champions.

15 // **August**

> Alain Giresse (left) and Lothar Matthäus battle for the ball, while Luis Fernandez (right) writhes on the ground after being fouled by Wolfgang Rolff (second from right).
< Manuel Amoros (right) and Andreas Brehme during the semifinal France vs. Germany (0–2).

Once again, no glory for France, the most proficient European team in the 1980s. As in 1982, the Equipe Tricolore faltered in the semifinal because of Germany's robustness and France's own nervousness—this time due to goalkeeper Joël Bats reacting wrongly to a free kick by Andreas Brehme. Germany held them at bay for eighty minutes, and Rudi Völler compounded their frustration by sealing France's fate with a last-minute goal. It marked the beginning of a twelve-year lean period for the reigning European champions and their star, Michel Platini. Twice France failed to qualify for the World Cup. But finally, in 1998, in their own country and under the auspices of Platini, who no longer played as a striker but orchestrated a championship, France was compensated for its run of bad luck in the 1980s. ⚽

1986 // Mexico

16 // August

> **William Ayache (left) and Patrick Battiston,**
France's defensive bulwark, during the
quarterfinal against Germany.

No revenge for Patrick Battiston (middle), and no hard feelings either. The Frenchman had been fouled brutally by German goalkeeper Toni Schumacher in 1982, suffering two lost teeth and a cracked cervical vertebra. However, four years later, he didn't get his payback against Germany, as some people undoubtedly had hoped. Unlike many of his fellow countrymen, who had been outraged at Schumacher's cynical offer to "pay for the jacket crowns," Battiston always took a conciliatory view. While Schumacher was dumped from the national team following the publication of his garrulous book *Anpfiff* (*Kickoff*) and found himself marginalized, Battiston is, to this day, a role model of reliability, modesty, and fair play. In the space of eighteen years he played in 530 first division games, was European champion, and was French champion on five occasions. Later he headed the youth academy at Girondins de Bordeaux, which spawned the world champions Bixente Lizarazu and Christophe Dugarry. ⚽

> In spite of some amazing saves, Belgian goalkeeper Jean-Marie Pfaff ends up conceding four goals while vying for third place against France.

< Enzo Scifo (Belgium) during the Small Final.

"What's so special about Maradona?" Jean-Marie Pfaff had mouthed, prior to the semifinal, in an attempt to bring the Argentinean star down a few pegs after all the raving commentaries. But then Maradona showed the Belgian goalkeeper what was special about him and shot two goals. So the Belgians and their amazing, if somewhat boastful, goal-keeper—the surprise team of the tournament, who'd beaten the Soviet Union and Spain—ended up vying for third place with France, the greatest achievement in the soccer annals of this small country. ⚽

18 // August

....

....

....

....

....

Political leaders, presidents, and heads of state show up for World Cup finals. They want to cash in on the publicity and national prestige soccer can bestow before returning to the complicated and largely bland business of politics. It's easier for soccer professionals: the diplomatic rigmarole boils down to a captain's handshake, the exchange of pennants, and a few friendly words. After that, all that counts are deeds, goals, and hard facts. ⚽

1986 // Mexico

19 // **August**

> In a four-man struggle with goalkeeper Nery Pumpido and the Argentinean defense, German striker Rudi Völler seems to vanish.

< Maradona, at the center of the action (as always) between Karl-Heinz Förster (left) and Andreas Brehme.

1986 // Mexico

Supremacy up high, rather than on the turf, is often what clinches a match. Not surprisingly, air combat around Argentina's goal was fierce during the World Cup final. German striker Rudi Völler fought in an unsuccessful attempt to get past airborne defender José Luis Brown (front), Ruggeri, and the Argentinean goalkeeper Nery Pumpido. Pumpido then punched the ball and had the edge over his German counterpart Toni Schumacher, who crashed to the ground empty-handed—symbolizing the Germans' predicament. Twenty-three minutes into the game, a garishly costumed Schumacher hurtled past an incoming free kick by Brown ("Like a yellow brimstone butterfly"—*Süddeutsche Zeitung*), thus putting Argentina in the lead. ⚽

20 // August

1986 // Mexico

Flying was another discipline at which he was unsurpassed: Diego Armando Maradona soars here so elegantly above his pursuer Karl-Heinz Förster and goalkeeper Toni Schumacher that any sculptor would be glad to have him as a model.

21 // August

> Not even Lothar Matthäus (left), shown here
on a sliding trip with Ditmar Jakobs, could stop
Maradona.

Soccer as obstacle course: during the championship final, neither Lothar Matthäus nor Karl-Heinz Förster—who took over Matthäus's special job of marking Maradona during the second half—could handle the Argentinean. At least the Germans lived up to their reputation of battling to the bitter end. They achieved what no other nation's players had ever managed to do in a World Cup final: as in 1954, they were able to equalize after lagging 0–2 behind their opponent. But unlike in 1954, when Rahn shot their last-minute 3–2 Miracle of Bern goal, it was Argentina that clinched the match in 1986—through Maradona, of course, not as finisher, but as the guy who set it up. With five minutes left, he cleared a window of opportunity for Jorge Luis Burruchaga. Schumacher emerged from his goal too late to prevent Argentina's 3–2 victory.

22 // August

> **Maradona, carrying the World Cup in his hands, is carried on the shoulders of the Argentinean fans.**

No other player has ever dominated a World Championship so completely. Never again did Maradona play as superbly as in 1986. But the euphoria he unleashed, the almost-religious veneration he encountered, proved too much for him. Drugs, heart problems, Mafia connections, rubbing shoulders with Fidel Castro, firing shots at journalists, tax debts: his life turned into a grotesque escapade. And still, no other soccer player ever engendered such a permanent sense of gratitude—and this in every corner of the world. In 2003 Gustavo Sierra, a reporter covering the Iraq War for the newspaper *Clarín*, described how Maradona saved his life after he was threatened by Iraqi gunmen. "They asked where we came from. I said: Argentina. And then, all of a sudden, they uttered the magic words: Argentina? Maradona! Their mood had changed, they started laughing and they let us go, without a scratch."

1990 // Italy

- 23 // August
> 24 // August

For Germany, the World Cup in Italy came at exactly the right time. Amid the euphoria of reunification, the victory parade of Franz Beckenbauer's team was the high point in a joint East-West celebration that would soon give way to the divisive realities of everyday life in the new Germany. While the joy of victory is what remained in the minds of the German public, for the rest of the world the competition was an unattractive, fairly boring affair. Brazil, known worldwide for its superb soccer, failed earlier than ever before. Italy and England complained of their bad luck with penalty kicks. And, with the exception of the refreshing performance of the Cameroons, the World Cup was dominated by very destructive, almost cynical play. Later FIFA took this as an opportunity to make several changes to the rules in hopes of restoring soccer to a more offensive, more constructive game. One change restricted the goalkeeper from picking up back passes. Other rules included expulsion for a foul by the last defensive player; tougher penalties for tackles from behind and therefore more protection for forwards; and the change that the position "level with the last two opponents" no longer counts as offside. Thus the World Cup in Italy proved to be a thought-provoking impetus for international soccer, helping ensure it wouldn't be caught offside when it came to popular interest.

ITALIA 90

FIRST ROUND, GROUP A

Italy vs. Austria 1–0
Czechoslovakia vs. USA 5–1
Italy vs. USA 1–0
Czechoslovakia vs. Austria 1–0
Italy vs. Czechoslovakia 2–0
Austria vs. USA 2–1

RESULTS
1. Italy (Points: 6, Goals: 4–0)
2. Czechoslovakia (4, 6–3)
3. Austria (2, 2–3)
4. USA (0, 2–8)

FIRST ROUND, GROUP B

Cameroon vs. Argentina 1–0
Romania vs. Soviet Union 2–0
Argentina vs. Soviet Union 2–0
Cameroon vs. Romania 2–1
Argentina vs. Romania 1–1
Soviet Union vs. Cameroon 4–0

RESULTS
1. Cameroon (Points: 4, Goals: 3–5)
2. Romania (3, 4–3)
3. Argentina (3, 3–2)
4. Soviet Union (2, 4–4)

FIRST ROUND, GROUP C

Brazil vs. Sweden 2–1
Costa Rica vs. Scotland 1–0
Brazil vs. Costa Rica 1–0
Scotland vs. Sweden 2–1
Brazil vs. Scotland 1–0
Costa Rica vs. Sweden 2–1

RESULTS
1. Brazil (Points: 6, Goals: 4–1)
2. Costa Rica (4, 3–2)
3. Scotland (2, 2–3)
4. Sweden (0, 3–6)

FIRST ROUND, GROUP D

Colombia vs. United Arab Emirates 2–0
Germany vs. Yugoslavia 4–1
Yugoslavia vs. Colombia 1–0
Germany vs. United Arab Emirates 5–1
Colombia vs. Germany 1–1
Yugoslavia vs. United Arab Emirates 4–1

RESULTS
1. Germany (Points: 5, Goals: 10–3)
2. Yugoslavia (4, 6–5)
3. Colombia (3, 3–2)
4. United Arab Emirates (0, 2–11)

FIRST ROUND, GROUP E

Belgium vs. South Korea 2–0
Uruguay vs. Spain 0–0
Belgium vs. Uruguay 3–1
Spain vs. South Korea 3–1
Spain vs. Belgium 2–1
Uruguay vs. South Korea 1–0

RESULTS
1. Spain (Points: 5, Goals: 5–2)
2. Belgium (4, 6–3)
3. Uruguay (3, 2–3)
4. South Korea (0, 1–6)

FIRST ROUND, GROUP F

England vs. Ireland 1–1
Holland vs. Egypt 1–1
Holland vs. England 0–0
Ireland vs. Egypt 0–0
England vs. Egypt 1–0
Holland vs. Ireland 1–1

RESULTS
1. England (Points: 4, Goals: 2–1)
2. Holland (3, 2–2)
3. Ireland (3, 2–2)
4. Egypt (2, 1–2)

ROUND OF SIXTEEN

Cameroon vs. Colombia 2–1 OT
Czechoslovakia vs. Costa Rica 4–1
Argentina vs. Brazil 1–0
Germany vs. Holland 2–1
Ireland vs. Romania 5–4 PEN
Italy vs. Uruguay 2–0
Yugoslavia vs. Spain 2–1 OT
England vs. Belgium 1–0 OT

QUARTERFINALS

Argentina vs. Yugoslavia 3–2 PEN
Italy vs. Ireland 1–0
Germany vs. Czechoslovakia 1–0
England vs. Cameroon 3–2 OT

SEMIFINALS

Argentina vs. Italy 5–4 PEN
Germany vs. England 5–4 PEN

THIRD-PLACE MATCH

Italy vs. England 2–1

FINAL

Germany vs. Argentina 1–0

World Cup Champion: GERMANY

25 // August

Diego in a double-decker. Here, soccer star Maradona is stuck between a rock and a hard place—just like his team, titleholder Argentina. Since 1962, all opening games had ended without a single goal. Until 1990. Then, the first goal was in the first game—by Cameroon: the tally ended 1–0 for the underdogs, the world champions defeated. Thus, after just the first day, the World Cup already was offering rich emotional stuff: a lot of gloating over Argentina's loss and a new pride in soccer for the Africans.

1990 // Italy

26 // August

Two millionaires in one house: Here, the oil tycoon Massimo Moratti (right), boss of Inter Milan, and the media entrepreneur Silvio Berlusconi, owner of AC Milan and later Italian prime minister, look content under the new roof of the Guiseppe Meazza (San Siro) Stadium. The shared playing field of the two traditional Milan clubs was, like many other arenas, newly refurbished just for the World Cup—something that the clubs and fans (and, of course, the owners) profited from long after the championship was over.

1990 // Italy

27 **//** August

> **Model of dependability and high standards:**
Paolo Maldini played from 1990 until 2002 in four
World Cups for Italy.

The picture of youth: ageless Paolo Maldini at his first World Cup. Twelve years later, after the 2002 World Cup, he would finish his international career as the Italian national record holder, having played in 126 games. But this was by no means the end of his club career. In January 1985, at the age of sixteen, he had taken part in his first game in the Serie A. In March 2005, his contract was renewed until 2007. Thus, in over twenty years and over seven hundred games—all with AC Milan—he won the European Cup four times and seven national championship titles. In 1994, he was the first defender to be chosen Soccer Player of the Year. In a soccer world in which careers are becoming increasingly short-lived, Paolo Maldini is the personification of dependability and club loyalty. ⚽

28 // August

Modern-day humans only need their heads to think—and, of course, to coordinate the movements of other parts of the body. It's different in soccer: the head is also used as a tool. Because the hand is not permitted for use in the game, you need your head to do the work in an area that your foot cannot reach: it has to think and do headers, too. But according to scientific studies, none of this is particularly healthy for the good old gray matter. On the average, a professional player performs eight hundred headers per season, some defensive players as many as twenty-five hundred. It's no wonder that this constant battering affects many players' short-term memories. But at least the important goals end up as lasting memories for millions of fans. ⚽

29 // August

Past and present: against Spain, Uruguay had to contend with a 0–0 draw, before eventually being eliminated by Italy after lackluster performances in the round of sixteen. Sixty years after winning the title in Montevideo and forty years after triumphing in Rio, the first-ever World Cup champion had become mired in modern-day mediocrity. It would take twelve years before Uruguay was able to qualify again for the World Championship. ⚽

30 // August

> **Oleg Kuznetzov (left) and José Tiburci**
Serrizuela during the 2–0 confrontation
Argentina vs. Soviet Union.

Ball ballet: the dance with the ball produces moments of great elegance, not visible in the action-packed dynamics of the game itself, but revealed by the lens of a high-speed camera. Here, the Argentinean player José Tiburci Serrizuela seems to have the tango in his blood, while his opponent Oleg Kuznetzov counters with the grace of a Russian ballet dancer—a one-on-one confrontation in the form of a cross-cultural pas de deux.

1990 // Italy

31 // August

Here's looking at you, kid: Argentinean goalkeeper Sergio Goycoechea, unable to reach the ball, seems to will its path to change by applying hypnotic powers. Though there's scientific evidence that this technique doesn't work with balls, it does sometimes work when applied to soccer players: facing penalty kicks from Yugoslavia and Italy, Goycoechea was able to stop five out of ten shots, bringing his team into the final. ⚽

1990 // Italy

1 // September

> Ricardo Ferri (Italy, left) one-on-one with
Bruce Murray (USA).
< Giuseppe Giannini (Italy) and his opponent
John Doyle (USA, right).

Keeping him grounded: being a modern-day defensive player, Italian Riccardo Ferri knows that arms can help when legs are too slow. Grabbing hold of the American Bruce Murray, he makes sure that the elegantly airborne player doesn't get very far—and in doing so seems to guide him like a puppeteer steering his puppet. Giuseppe Giannini and John Doyle (photo left) also seem intent on demonstrating how arms and hands can be useful in soccer: using a technique common in children's playgrounds, they strive for the ball. ⚽

1990 // Italy

2 // September

The world of work is unfair, not just in the office: one guy toils, while another gets the credit. That's what it's like in soccer, too: strikers are remembered for their goals, not their missed opportunities. Goalkeepers, on the other hand, are rated by the mistakes they make: they are always remembered for bad, rather than good, performances. During the 1990 World Cup, Walter Zenga made just one mistake: after five games and 517 minutes of play (a World Cup record!), he failed to prevent Caniggia (Argentina) from scoring the equalizer in the semifinal. Host and favorite Italy went down on penalties. Zenga will always be remembered for this one unlucky moment, rather than the thousands of saves he had notched up. ⚽

3 // September

The volcanic activity of Etna, Vesuvius, or Stromboli are nothing compared to the joyful eruptions of Italian scorers. Giuseppe Giannini has every reason to be euphoric, and at this point he doesn't even realize that his 12th-minute goal is the one that will secure victory in this 1–0 confrontation. It will remain the only goal in the qualifying round against the USA. ⚽

1990 // Italy

4 // September

> Giving his best, Austrian Anton Pfeffer back-tackles Tomas Skuhravy, but in the end the hard work doesn't pay off: Czechoslovakia wins 1–0.

They were the inventors of Danube Soccer: between the World Wars, the capitals of the old Austro-Hungarian Empire—Vienna, Prague, and Budapest—boasted the most technically proficient football in Europe. Half a century later, Austrian and Czechoslovakian teams were no better than average in their games—and Hungary even failed to qualify for the championship. ⚽

5 // September

....

....

....

....

....

Soccer is peace? This promise, proclaimed on banners in English and Flemish during the match between Belgium and Uruguay (3–1), has not always been fulfilled. In 1969, riots at the World Cup qualifier between El Salvador and Honduras led to the so-called Soccer War between these nations. Three thousand people were killed. But soccer's main stage, the World Cup, has remained for the most part free of major hostilities.

1990 // Italy

6 // September

A figure like someone out of an adventure movie and a hairstyle that might have been borrowed from a Pippi Longstocking book: Carlos Valderrama, visually the most eccentric player in all three of his World Cups. In the round of sixteen in 1990, the Colombian with the lion's mane faced Cameroon, the team that called itself the Unbeatable Lions. And, indeed, they roared the loudest, winning 2–1 in overtime, making them the first African team to reach the World Cup quarterfinals. ⚽

7 // September

Roger Milla already was able to look back on a successful career and was in semi-retirement, playing a bit of soccer on Reunion Island. But then the powers that be remembered him and took him along to the World Cup in Italy. It was the beginning of a soccer legend. Milla shot two goals against Romania and enthralled the soccer world with his jubilant behavior: a thirty-eight-year-old hip-swinging around the corner flag as if it were a beautiful woman. He was able to repeat this dance twice during the match against Colombia in the round of sixteen. First he scored 1–0 in overtime, then he snatched the ball from under the nose of Colombia's keeper René Higuita, whacking it into the empty goal for a 2–0 finish. Cameroon was the first African team to reach a World Cup quarter-final, where it was only just beaten by England. In 1994 Milla became the oldest World Cup scorer ever. After that, it was finally time for him to retire from professional soccer.

8 // September

> Faith can move mountains, or goals, as the case may be: the Brazilians are unable to score. Maradona and his team triumph, more through luck than anything else, by scoring in the 80th minute.

< Argentinean Pedro Monzon (left) one-on-one with Brazil's Careca.

Heavenly help: Diego Maradona prays for assistance from above. And this wish was duly granted when Argentina scored 1–0 against a superior Brazilian team. But Argentina's coach, Carlos Bilardo, didn't want to rely solely on divine intervention and devised what could literally be described as a sick scheme: during a pause in the game, he slipped the Brazilian player Branco a bottle of water laced with a sleeping pill. Branco said later he couldn't play properly after drinking it.

9 // September

At the height of their careers, Marco van Basten and Ruud Gullit were the best strikers in Europe. In the European Championship in 1988, they led Holland to victory with two dream goals. Playing for Milan, they dominated the Italian championship and the European Cup. But in the World Cup they never were able to demonstrate their true caliber. In 1986 Holland failed to qualify. In 1990, handicapped by strife within the team, Holland went on to defeat in spite of their stars' valiant efforts (three draws in the qualifying round followed by a defeat to Germany). And in 1994 the world championship took place without these brilliant strikers. Van Basten was forced to retire due to a knee injury. And Gullit, as captain, fell out with coach Dick Advocaat, deserted his team, and went home. ⚽

> Dutch player Frank Rijkaard, the Llama, grabs German striker Rudi Völler's hair.

< The tension shows during the round-of-sixteen match Germany vs. Holland 2–1: goalkeeper Hans van Breukelen quarrels with Rudi Völler (No. 9).

Soccer's a game that gets bodily fluids churning. Sweat flows, blood seethes, everything's in motion. "The Footeball (soccer) strengtheneth and brawneth the whole body, and by provoking superfluities downeward, it dischargeth the head, and upper partes"—Richard Mulcaster, a contemporary of Shakespeare, knew this already. But occasionally, it's the wrong fluids that are mobilized, especially when two teams, or two players, don't get along: adrenalin-soaked aggression, and sometimes even saliva. This is what happened with Frank Rijkaard, who earned his nickname, "the Llama," when he spat on Rudi Völler. He clearly deserved the red card—unlike Rudi Völler, who was also given one. This was the low point of the seething German-Dutch soccer rivalry, a relationship that has since become more civilized, as is only fitting for neighboring countries.

11 // September

....

....

....

....

....

While the mood in Germany displayed odd touches of national chauvinism ("Send him back to the pampa," German TV commentator Heribert Fassbender demanded, meaning the Argentinean referee), the Swabian's son Jürgen Klinsmann remained, as always, diplomatic and focused on essentials during the group-of-sixteen match against Holland—the essential thing being to score. Through his leading goal and Andreas Brehme's artful score, the Germans got their revenge for Hamburg 1988. Back then, Germany had been defeated in the semifinal of the European Cup, and Dutchman Ronald Koeman had theatrically wiped his behind with a German jersey following the shirt swap. This time around, however, Klinsmann showed everyone how it should be done: wear it and rejoice! ⚽

12 // September

Dreams of the Emerald Isle: for two weeks, twelve thousand Irish fans dotted the Italian islands of Sicily and Sardinia with their nation's color, euphorically celebrating three draws in matches against England, Egypt, and Holland, taking Ireland, for the first time ever, beyond the World Cup's qualifying rounds. In their round-of-sixteen clash with Romania, the Irish still didn't score. But after this goalless two-hour confrontation, the rules demanded a victor: through penalty kicking. Ireland won this mental trial when goal-keeper Pat Bonner saved against Daniel Timofte, and the team triumphed in Genoa. But the run of fortune ended five days later when the Irish played against Italy in Rome. Nevertheless, Ireland was one of the few teams that made a splash during this World Championship and will be remembered for that.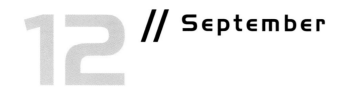

> John Barnes, plowing through during the round-of-sixteen game against Belgium, which England won 1–0.

< An English fan waving the Union Jack.

John Barnes was a controversial figure for some, the first black player donning an English team jersey. He was the first of many players within European soccer to represent the modern face of society, the national teams (especially of the former colonial powers) reflecting their countries' cultural diversity. Doing so, they are sometimes confronted with the latent (or even blatant) racism that certain people seem to feel a need to display when they enter a soccer stadium. ⚽

14 // September

A flank, a jump, a header into the net, followed by a wild victory sprint, eyes beaming into the cameras: the most penetrating glance in world soccer. The history of the 1990 World Cup is, above all, the history of a short guy from Messina, the only southern Italian on the host nation's team, teasingly called *terrone* (earth eater) by his colleagues. With his six goals in seven games, he became the darling of the nation, especially the south, the Mezzogiorno, which finally had its hero. Salvatore Schillaci, also known as Toto, scored again and again—as in the semifinal against Argentina. But that goal proved to be the last in Sicily's goal spree.

15 // September

1990 // Italy

Rude awakening after a summer dream: after five successive victories without conceding a goal, all of Italy was anticipating a glorious final. Then the spoilsports struck. Diego Maradona shot a brilliant pass to Julio Olarticoechea, freeing him on the wing, flanking the ball to Claudio Caniggia, who scored the 1–1 equalizer, which Argentina defended to the final whistle. Maradona triumphed over goalkeeper Zenga in the penalty shoot-out, while Italy's Roberto Donadoni and Aldo Serena lost in the battle of nerves. The country's World Cup ambitions were thwarted.

16 // September

Great operas need heroes, great movies need tears. Great soccer can offer both: tearful heroes. Paul Gascoigne shed tears after getting the yellow card for fouling German Thomas Berthold during the semifinal. At that moment he knew his dream of reaching the final was over: even if England were to enter the last round, he wouldn't be on the team. Gascoigne was one of the great new talents to emerge at the World Cup in 1990, and the young man's spontaneous outburst touched the hearts of his fellow countrymen. To this day, it is regarded as one of the most poignant moments in English soccer history. In the end, England lost after a nerve-wracking battle in overtime, followed by a penalty showdown. After that, Gascoigne wasn't the only one with tears in his eyes.

17 // September

> **> Duel of the captains: Lothar Matthäus and Diego Maradona (right) during the World Cup final, Germany vs. Argentina.**
> **< The Olympic Stadium in Rome, venue for the World Cup final on July 1, 1990.**

Soccer as a shadow play. Effective man-to-man marking means sticking to your opponent as though you were his shadow—as was done with Diego Maradona. During the World Cup final, he always had a counterpart, usually Guido Buchwald, sometimes Lothar Matthäus. The German captain stayed glued to the Argentinean captain so that Germany wouldn't suffer the same fate as the Brazilians and Italians: a few quick magic tricks with the ball and then, game over. In this final, the Argentinean magician didn't get a chance. ⚽

18 // September

Four Argentinean players were barred from the final, and key player Maradona was not at full strength. So handicapped Argentina adopted a destructive strategy against Germany. In the end it had two fewer men on the field and complained that the referee had treated the team unfairly, especially when it came to the penalty kick that clinched the game. ⚽

1990 // Italy

19 // September

In soccer, nicknames are given to popular players. In Germany, the attribute is usually conferred by the letter "i" at the end of the name. In the 1990 World Cup the German team boasted four such players: Rudi (Völler), Andi (Brehme), Klinsi (Klinsmann), and Litti (Littbarski). Less frequently, players are named after the greats of the game. FC Zurich adopted a young bull as a mascot, whom they called Maradona. (Once, this Maradona stampeded onto the pitch, forcing the players to flee.) The German player Guido Buchwald was similarly honored during the 1990 World Cup. After the brilliant goal that gave Germany the lead over Holland, he was given the first name of the soccer maestro, of the man he was to cover during the final: Guido Buchwald became Diego Buchwald. ⚽

20 // September

> The score is still 0-0. Rudi Völler (left) and Oscar Ruggeri during the World Cup final, Germany vs. Argentina.

A flying performance worthy of an Oscar: Rudi Völler in a diagonal acrobatic stance, confronted by his determined opponent Oscar Ruggeri. It was one of the many chances the German team had to score, but in the end the Germans clinched their third World Cup victory after a controversial late penalty.

1990 // Italy

21 // September

> Andreas Brehme's perfectly executed shot is unreachable for Argentina's goalkeeper Sergio Goycoechea.

< Eighty-five minutes into the game: the decisive penalty, converted by Andreas Brehme.

The ball was in the net, the decisive moment in this World Cup. If someone up in space had pointed an ear at the Earth, he would have heard, in this split-second, the massive eruption: cheering, groaning, lamenting, screaming—the whole gamut of emotions from ecstasy to grief. All in this brief moment, as Andreas Brehme's perfectly shot missile whizzed past the left post and into the net, and goalkeeper Sergio Goycoechea was still in flight, not yet aware of his failure. It was the moment in which the tension that had been building up for weeks was released in a global outburst. ⚽

22 // September

> Pierre Littbarski, Stefan Reuter, Rudi Völler, and Jürgen Klinsmann (right to left) hurl toward Andreas Brehme.

< A little kiss for the scorer, from the German No. 9, Rudi Völler.

1990 // Italy

Millionaire's embrace. The whole crowd of handsomely paid colleagues piles on top of scorer Andreas Brehme. He enjoys this triumphant gesture, even though the final whistle is still minutes away. But at this moment everyone already realizes that this was the deciding goal: Germany is the 1990 World Cup champion.

23 // September

The final whistle that ends the dream. Only two reigning world champions were able to defend their titles during the preceding seventy-five years: Italy in 1938 and Brazil in 1962. Argentina failed in 1990. Diego Armando Maradona, the greatest soccer player of his time, perhaps even of the century, is devastated by the realization that fame and glory are fleeting things. ⚽

24 // September

> Fame to those that deserve it: team manager Franz Beckenbauer celebrating with, and being celebrated by, his team.

< Reception for the team at the Frankfurt Römer. German fans giving their triumphant team a roaring welcome after the players return home.

Emperor Franz as King Midas: in the world of kids' comics, Gladstone Gander always has luck on his side. In the world of soccer, the lucky devil is Franz Beckenbauer. Whatever he touched would turn to gold. As a player, he won the World Cup in 1974, as team manager, he won it in 1990. And as leading German soccer functionary, he succeeded in winning the bid for the 2006 world championship. ⚽

1990 // Italy

25 // September

> Object of desire for all national team players: German captain Lothar Matthäus, having won the right to kiss the trophy.

The magic of the night. Here, Lothar Matthäus presses his lips on the most kissable object in the soccer world: the World Cup trophy, which sits waiting in a vault until it is handed to the new victor. After several days, the remnants of saliva, sweat, and champagne are removed and it is polished, destined to return to its resting place, where it will have to wait another four years before being retrieved for yet another round of kisses.

1990 // Italy

1994 // U.S.

- 26 // September
- 27 // September

It is the year A.D. **1994**. The whole world is ruled by King Soccer. The whole world? Not quite: one particularly obstinate nation has resisted its rule and prefers to devote its attention to athletes who, rather than chasing a round, air-filled ball, haggle for an egg-shaped object, or throw and catch a smaller orb, hitting it with a bat. So in 1994, the soccer empire boldly set its sights on the basketball-, football-, and baseball-crazed U.S. But nobody can claim that the Americans simply ignored the game the rest of the

world prefers: American households tuned in, with 3.75 million viewers (a million more than in 1990), an average of 68,600 per match—that's a record for American viewership of World Cup soccer. And the rule changes introduced after the somewhat lame 1990 championships to encourage a more offensive style of soccer had their effect: on average, there were 2.7 goals per match, up half a point per game from 1990. And yet, one couldn't help but get the impression that the spark of enthusiasm didn't quite ignite the hearts and minds of the nation. True: a foundation was laid for soccer as an acceptable discipline within the realm of youth, college, and women's sport. But the average American remains passionately committed to basketball, football, and baseball. And so the soccer circus moved on to places where King Soccer rules supreme.

FIRST ROUND, GROUP A

USA vs. Switzerland 1–1
Romania vs. Colombia 3–1
Switzerland vs. Romania 4–1
USA vs. Colombia 2–1
Romania vs. USA 1–0
Colombia vs. Switzerland 2–0

RESULTS
1. Romania (Points: 6, Goals: 5–5)
2. Switzerland (4, 5–4)
3. USA (4, 3–3)
4. Colombia (3, 4–5)

FIRST ROUND, GROUP B

Cameroon vs. Sweden 2–2
Brazil vs. Russia 2–0
Brazil vs. Cameroon 3–0
Sweden vs. Russia 3–1
Russia vs. Cameroon 6–1
Brazil vs. Sweden 1–1

RESULTS
1. Brazil (Points: 7, Goals: 6–1)
2. Sweden (5, 6–4)
3. Russia (3, 7–6)
4. Cameroon (1, 3–11)

FIRST ROUND, GROUP C

Germany vs. Bolivia 1–0
Spain vs. South Korea 2–2
Germany vs. Spain 1–1
South Korea vs. Bolivia 0–0
Spain vs. Bolivia 3–1
Germany vs. South Korea 3–2

RESULTS
1. Germany (Points: 7, Goals: 5–3)
2. Spain (5, 6–4)
3. South Korea (2, 4–5)
4. Bolivia (1, 1–4)

FIRST ROUND, GROUP D

Argentina vs. Greece 4–0
Nigeria vs. Bulgaria 3–0
Argentina vs. Nigeria 2–1
Bulgaria vs. Greece 4–0
Nigeria vs. Greece 2–0
Bulgaria vs. Argentina 2–0

RESULTS
1. Nigeria (Points: 6, Goals: 6–2)
2. Bulgaria (6, 6–3)
3. Argentina (6, 6–3)
4. Greece (0, 0–10)

FIRST ROUND, GROUP E

Ireland vs. Italy 1–0
Norway vs. Mexico 1–0
Italy vs. Norway 1–0
Mexico vs. Ireland 2–1
Ireland vs. Norway 0–0
Italy vs. Mexico 1–1

RESULTS
1. Mexico (Points: 4, Goals: 3–3)
2. Ireland (4, 2–2)
3. Italy (4, 2–2)
4. Norway (4, 1–1)

FIRST ROUND, GROUP F

Belgium vs. Morocco 1–0
Holland vs. Saudi Arabia 2–1
Belgium vs. Holland 1–0
Saudi Arabia vs. Morocco 2–1
Holland vs. Morocco 2–1
Saudi Arabia vs. Belgium 1–0

RESULTS
1. Holland (Points: 6, Goals: 4–3)
2. Saudi Arabia (6, 4–3)
3. Belgium (6, 2–1)
4. Morocco (0, 2–5)

ROUND OF SIXTEEN

Germany vs. Belgium 3–2
Spain vs. Switzerland 3–0
Sweden vs. Saudi Arabia 3–1
Romania vs. Argentina 3–2
Holland vs. Ireland 2–0
Brazil vs. USA 1–0
Italy vs. Nigeria 2–1 OT
Bulgaria vs. Mexico 4–2 PEN

QUARTERFINALS

Italy vs. Spain 2–1
Brazil vs. Holland 3–2
Bulgaria vs. Germany 2–1
Sweden vs. Romania 7–6 PEN

SEMIFINALS

Italy vs. Bulgaria 2–1
Brazil vs. Sweden 1–0

THIRD-PLACE MATCH

Sweden vs. Bulgaria 4–0

FINAL

Brazil vs. Italy 3–2 PEN

World Cup Champion: BRAZIL

28 // September

Greek columns and American skyscrapers: the soccer world was in for some surprises when it ventured to the land of unlimited architectural opportunities. For instance: the architecture and visuals within Chicago's Soldier Field. The seventy-year-old arena, with its classical Greek columns—usually the home of the National Football League's Chicago Bears—was host to the opening ceremony of the 1994 World Cup and to five games, three of them with the reigning champions, Germany.

1994 // U.S.

29 // September

> Opening ceremony for the 1994 World Cup:
colored balloons rise into the sky above Chicago.
< American soul legend Diana Ross performing at
the opening ceremony in Soldier Field.

The 1994 World Cup opening ceremony, a varied program that included two curious events: the first person injured during the championship was U.S. singer Jon Secada—and that without placing a foot on the playing field. The pop star had just started performing the song "If You Go" at the opening ceremony in Chicago when the stage collapsed and he disappeared in front of a billion TV viewers worldwide. The luckless Secada continued singing from underneath the stage before he was taken to the hospital, where he was diagnosed as having a dislocated shoulder. The first miss of the tournament can be attributed to Secada's fellow artist Diana Ross, also during the opening bash. Apart from performing music, she was supposed to usher in the games by kicking a ball into the net. But even though she was only a short distance away, she missed the goal. ⚽

"I am nothing more than a beggar for good soccer," wrote the poet and soccer lover Eduardo Galeano. "So I travel the world, cap in hand, and in the stadiums I beg aloud: just one brilliant move, God willing." Indeed, the player who satisfies the desire of millions, their longing for enthralling soccer, is called the king. And thus, the player who scores most goals is dubbed the King of Goals. The Russian Oleg Salenko shot six goals during the 1994 World Cup, five of those during the last group game against Cameroon, his team already having failed to qualify for the next round. No one else in the sixty-four-year history of the World Cup had ever scored as many goals in a single game. But he had to share this fame with Hristo Stoitchkov, who also scored six times, though more evenly spread across the tournament: thanks to him, Bulgaria reached the semifinal. ⚽

1 // **October**

> Jürgen Klinsmann scores to clinch the World Cup's first three-point victory (after FIFA began awarding three points, instead of two, for a win).

End of a series: since 1974, the reigning champions always played in the opening games of the World Cup, but they never went on to win. Germany changed this pattern in 1994, Jürgen Klinsmann scoring a goal for a 1–0 win over Bolivia. ⚽

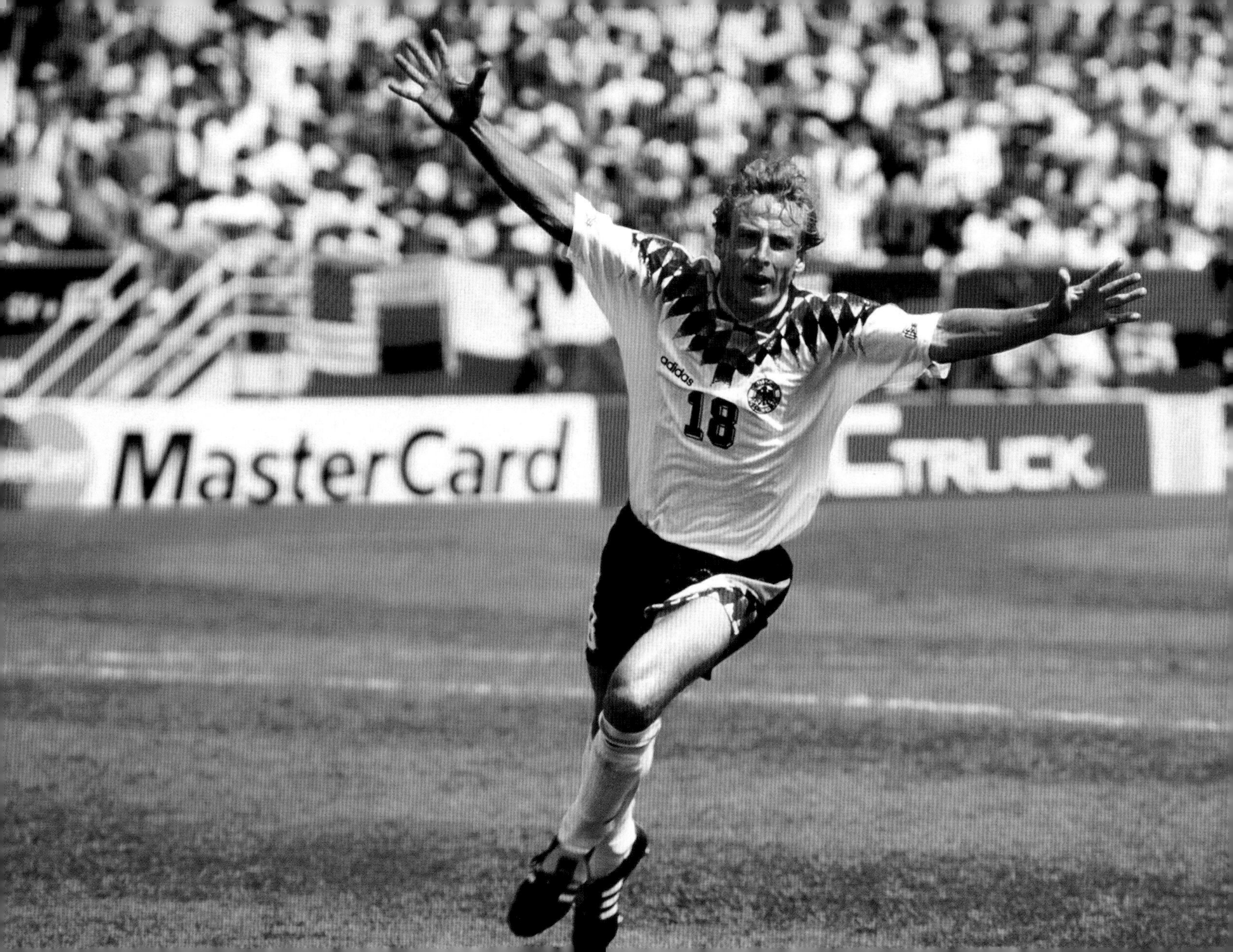

adidas
18
MasterCard
TRUCK

2 // October

> The soccer World Cup in the football-mad U.S.: in New York and other cities, the matches were held in football arenas.

1994 // U.S.

The Big Apple awaits the little ball around which the whole World Cup revolves. Pelé, Franz Beckenbauer, and other aging megastars had played for the New York Cosmos in the North American Soccer League in the 1970s, generating initial enthusiasm in this capital of world capitals. But even in New York, the world's most popular game was thwarted by the popularity of baseball and football. That didn't change in 1994, when seven World Cup matches were held in New York's Giants Stadium.

3 // October

Soccer under a dome: the meeting between host USA and Switzerland was the first match in World Cup history to take place indoors. Twenty-two players and 73,425 spectators were sheltered from the 104-degree heat and high humidity outside as they watched the teams play in the Pontiac Silverdome in Detroit. The game also lacked fresh air, with the match ending at a weary 1–1.

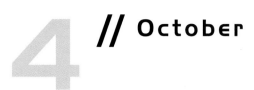

4 // October

> Beaming with joy after the fortunate winning goal: Dutch player Dennis Bergkamp (right) hugs scorer Gaston Taument.

The living desert: for eighty-five minutes Saudi Arabia, the underdog guest from the Middle East, proved to be the better team. But then the Saudi goalkeeper Al-Deayea committed a serious error, and the Dutch favorites accepted the gift, shooting the 2–1 winning goal. Here, Dennis Bergkamp is able to embrace his teammate and goalkeeper Gaston Taument with a sigh of relief—the relief of the favorite who was only just able to avoid disgrace. ⚽

5 // October

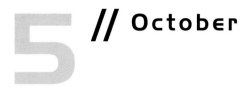

A first-class flight: Stefan Effenberg dives in front of goalkeeper Andoni Zubizarreta to make sure Jürgen Klinsmann's header lands beyond the line for a 1–1 final score between Germany and Spain. However, in the following group match against South Korea he showed less than exemplary composure: as he is subbed out and several fans boo him, he insults them with an obscene gesture. As a result, he is sent home by the German Football Association. It is only the third time in German World Cup history that a player is thrown off the squad: after Siggi Haringer in 1934, because he ate an orange on the train platform (which to national coach Otto Nerz showed an uncivil lack of discipline), and after Uli Stein, who claimed in 1986 that Adidas and not Beckenbauer put his rival Schumacher in goal. ⚽

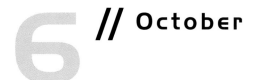

6 // October

"Fatal mistake": sports journalists often use flowery language to describe what, in the end, are nothing more than trivial incidents. But in the case of Andres Escobar, this choice of words was, unfortunately, all too accurate. The defender had shot an own goal during a 1–2 loss against the USA and thus was partly responsible for the Colombians being eliminated. While USA was celebrating after the final whistle, vengeance was being planned already in Colombia. Colombian soccer had been infiltrated long before by the cocaine Mafia, which laundered money in soccer clubs and also earned money in fraudulent betting. In 1989, a referee who was unwilling to go along with the Mafia's plans was murdered in cold blood. Not surprisingly, Escobar also expected the revenge of the Mafia. Eleven days after his mistake he was shot dead in a parking lot in Medellín. ⚽

1994 // U.S.

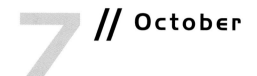

7 // October

The continents didn't shift after all: following Cameroon's spectacular performance in 1990 and Brazil's early elimination, many experts had predicted a new era in which Africa would overtake South America in soccer. However, in 1994 Brazil set the record straight again and dominated 3–0 against the Africans. While Brazil went on to become world champion, Cameroon was eliminated without a win during the qualifiers. But the Africans took two records home with them: the oldest player and oldest scorer in World Cup history (Roger Milla at forty-two years of age) and the youngest player to be sent off the field in World Cup action (seventeen-year-old Rigobert Song against Brazil).

8 // October

The last cocktail: just as he had done in the 4–0 win against Greece, the soccer genius Diego Armando Maradona gave a brilliant performance against Nigeria, setting up the 2–1 winning goal with a mean free kick. However, after the game, the soccer world was hit by some shocking news: Maradona had failed a drug test. Five different kinds of stimulants had been found in his urine—the leftovers of a cocktail containing weight loss pills that he had taken to get back down to World Cup weight after too many excesses. For the man who was once the greatest soccer player in the world, it was the end of an exceptional career—and the beginning of a long road of diets and drug rehabilitation programs, of financial, personal, physical, and psychological lows. ⚽

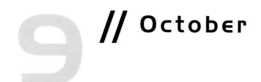

9 // October

Goalkeepers are supposed to be spotless. When they manage to maintain the necessary hygiene, they are happily praised for keeping their box clean, or keeping a "clean sheet." Clearing the ball with his goal kick in Soldier Field in Chicago, Borislav Mikhailov maintained a remarkably clean goal area. Because he also didn't allow any dirt in his work area in the remaining ninety minutes, Bulgaria won against Greece and celebrated its first victory at a World Cup following six World Cup appearances and seventeen total games. Because victory was so sweet, Bulgaria continued on its rampage, won the next three games, and reached the semifinals—with clean performances. ⚽

1994 // U.S.

Music, please: soccer players don't need instruments, because they have the ball. But soccer fans like to have something in their hands so they can demonstrate where their sentiments lie. Apparently unaware of this tradition, the American authorities initially refused to allow World Cup fans to take musical instruments into the stadium. After all, for their football and baseball fans, they would simply hire an organist to take care of the musical accompaniment. But finally the American organizers relented, and the Swiss didn't have to give up their cow bells, the Brazilians their samba drums, or the Koreans their gongs. ⚽

11 // October

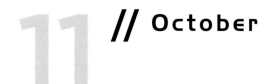

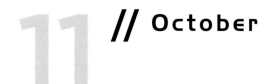 > Strong performance by Tzanko Tzvetanov (left), Krassimir Balakov, & Co.: the Bulgarians beat Argentina and reach the semifinals.

If only Diego Simeone (right) and Krassimir Balakov could jump that high: they have no chance against their own shadows. The evening sun in the Cotton Bowl in Dallas, Texas, threw particularly long shadows during the Bulgarians' 2–0 win against Argentina. ⚽

12 // October

"A bowl of cotton" is not exactly a promising name for a soccer stadium. But the Cotton Bowl, whose architecturally unusual silhouette does its best to stand out from the powerful skyline of the oil boomtown Dallas, saw a number of high-scoring games (twenty-three goals in six games), including the most exciting quarterfinal, Brazil against Holland 3–2.

1994 // U.S.

13 // October

> The Belgian Enzo Scifo exhausted and disappointed after the elimination of his team in the round of sixteen.

When the soccer field turns into a lawn for sunbathing, a defeat is usually to blame: here the Belgian Enzo Scifo is literally downtrodden after the 2–3 loss to Germany in the round of sixteen.

1994 // U.S.

14 // October

> Even Saeed Owairan, the first Middle Eastern
star, cannot prevent Saudi Arabia from falling
behind Sweden in the round of sixteen.

His great solo performance remained an exception: here, Saeed Owairan collapses in the face of the solid Swedish defense in the round of sixteen. Saudi Arabia went on to lose 1–3 to the Swedes, and all that remained for the best Arab player was the glory of having shot the most beautiful goal of the World Cup. This happened during the last group game against Belgium, when the Saudis needed a victory to advance. Owairan took care of it all by himself. He gained possession of the ball in his own half, stormed past four opposing players and shot a goal—right past Michel Preud'homme, the best goalkeeper of the tournament—to win 1–0. Saudi Arabia, the World Cup newcomer, had made it to the round of sixteen, and Middle Eastern soccer had a star for the first time. Owairan would definitely have been a hot item for European teams. But, until 1999, the all-powerful sheikhs prohibited the transfer of any Saudi player to a foreign country. ⚽

15 // October

The swish of the Divine Ponytail, as they called the their World Cup hero's hairdo back home in Italy. In the round of sixteen Roberto Baggio turned around a game that was considered already lost, shooting the equalizer just before the end against Nigeria and then netting the winning goal in overtime. He would later score the winning goal in the quarterfinal against Spain and even shoot both goals in the semifinal against Bulgaria. But then it all came to an end: penalty shots against Brazil, and the moment when Baggio's sights were set too high. ⚽

> In the round of sixteen, the Mexicans even brought down the opposing team's goal, but in the end they had to concede defeat to the Bulgarians.
< The Bulgarian Bontcho Guentchev outdoes Mexican goalkeeper Jorge Campos during penalties.

1994 // U.S.

In 1998, when a goal in Bernabéu Stadium collapsed during the Champions League semifinal between Real Madrid and Borussia Dortmund, it took the grounds crew one-and-a-half hours to set up a new one. A German TV commentator landed a classic of sports journalism when he dryly noted, "A goal would do the game some good." But in the 1994 World Cup, when the Mexican Marcelino Bernal fell into the Bulgarians' goal during the round of sixteen and took out the crossbar that held up the net, the workers in Giants Stadium demonstrated how things should really be done: they had a new goal standing in only seven minutes! The game lasted quite a bit longer than that, however—Bulgaria claimed the win only after overtime and penalties. ⚽

17 // October

> Lothar Matthäus, turned to stone, and Yordan
Letchkov just before takeoff: one man's facial
expression and another's gestures are all one
needs to figure out how the round-of-sixteen
match Germany vs. Bulgaria ended.
< Ilian Kiriakov (Bulgaria) and Guido Buchwald
(Germany, top) racing for the ball.

A picture says more than a thousand words: Captain Lothar Matthäus stands
frozen, the ball is in the net, and there's no goalkeeper in sight. The only action in the
picture is from the hero of the day, Yordan Letchkov. Here we can see him racing toward
his enthusiastic Bulgarian countrymen after heading the ball into the net for a spectacular 2–1 win over defending champion Germany.

18 // October

> They christened their sweeper after his great predecessor: Franco Baresi, nicknamed "Franz," during the 2–1 victory against Spain.

Originally, jersey numbers were something anonymous. When they were first used in the 1930s, they identified the position of a player in the tactical formation: 7 for the right wing, 9 for the center forward, and so on. But this soon came to an end. Increasingly, numbers came to be identified with players and not positions, and the lucrative business of selling jerseys to fans means making sure there's a connection between numbers and names. The greatest honor of all, however, is when a player's jersey number is retired with the player himself. This was the case with Franco Baresi, the legendary Italian defensive captain, who wore the number 6 for his country and his club. After he retired, AC Milan paid tribute to him by making his jersey immortal. No other players on the team are allowed to wear the number 6.

19 // October

Soccer has a heart for small people. Size may be important in basketball, handball, rugby, and football, but in soccer even the shortest player can be a star. Like Romário, who was also called Baixinho (little guy) back home in Brazil—a small, strapping goal scorer, just like Ferenc Puskás or Gerd Müller before him. Romário's ability to control the ball with the sole of his foot when dribbling has remained unmatched to this very day. The forward scored in five games, often in perfectly orchestrated teamwork with Bebeto. The two Brazilians also invented what may be the most original way to celebrate a goal in the World Cup: they would perform the Baby Cradle, pretending to rock to sleep the baby of the young father Bebeto in the quarterfinal against Holland. ⚽

1994 // U.S.

20 // October

Here, with the World Cup third-place medals around their necks, Stefan Schwarz and Henrik Larsson are cheered on by a crowd of ninety thousand in Pasadena, California. For title favorites, winning the so-called Small Final—the duel between the two semifinal losers—is rarely more than a consolation prize. For the underdog Sweden, however, the 4–0 against the tired Bulgarians was much more. "It's the all-time greatest accomplishment in Swedish soccer," said coach Tommy Svensson, whose team had been defeated only by the Brazilians. He considered third place in 1994 "better than second place in 1958, because since then the competition has gotten much stronger." ⚽

1994 // U.S.

21 // October

Goalless arena: although by game-time the goals had long since been set up, Pasadena's Rose Bowl experienced the first goalless final in World Cup history. The teams from Brazil and Italy didn't manage to put a ball into the net until the penalty shootout.

1994 // U.S.

22 // October

> Brazil's strong-running captain, Dunga (left), in a duel with the Italian Paolo Maldini.

< Roberto Baggio (Italy).

1994 // U.S.

When nobody wants to lose, the loser is the crowd. Between 1974 and 1990 the Brazilians shared their joy in the game with the entire world, but went on to lose each time. In 1994, however, they won their long-awaited fourth World Cup using European methods—with a team that was selected according to tactical discipline and stamina. Thus, in the final against Italy, they focused mainly on preventing goals. This effort was led by a captain who may not have been brilliant, but was strong-willed and a strong runner: Carlos Caetano Bledorn Verri, known as Dunga (the name of a dwarf in the Brazilian version of *Snow White*). The result was a lackluster final in which Brazil beat Italy 3–2 on penalties. But it was also Brazil's fourth World Cup title—and a sign that the South American team had abandoned soccer romanticism in favor of soccer realism.

23 // October

> The Brazilian Zinho (left) and the Italian Roberto Donadoni in one of more than two hundred duels per game, according to statistics.

Eleven versus eleven is only the surface of a soccer game. The true core is something else: man-on-man battles, multiplied hundreds of times. As a team sport, soccer consists of many individual duels. In fact, during the World Cup in 1994, statisticians counted an average of 205 per game; during the final, one of the more cautiously played matches, there were even more. Most coaches support the theory that a soccer game is won in these one-on-one battles. But sometimes the statistics tell another story: in the World Cup quarterfinal in 1998, the German national team won thirteen more one-on-one situations than the Croatians. But the Croatians shot three more goals.

1994 // U.S.

24 // October

The greatest goal scorer of all time, Pelé, called the penalty shot "the most cowardly form of shooting a goal." Maybe that was only an excuse to get out of shooting, because in this showdown beyond the choreography and drama of the team game, it is often the brilliant soccer players, the playmakers, and the great technicians who fail to perform. Sócrates and Platini missed penalty kicks in the 1986 World Cup quarterfinal between Brazil and France, and Zico had missed already in regulation time. In 1990 against Yugoslavia, Diego Maradona gave the most miserable shot of the World Cup. And then the final in 1994: after Brazilian goalkeeper Claudio Taffarel's save against Daniele Massaro, Roberto Baggio needed to score to keep Italy in the game. Baggio, an exceptionally skilled ball artist who had helped Italy to the final with five goals, ended up missing it, kicking his shot over the crossbar. ⚽

25 // October

Magic is part of Brazilian soccer: the team has been known to sprinkle salt on their opponent's territory and wheat or rice on its own. And in 1937, after a 0–12 loss to Vasco da Gama, a fan from Arubinha buried a toad whose mouth had been sewn shut beneath the field in Rio and uttered the curse: "Vasco will not win a championship for twelve years!" Brazil also attributed its first World Cup victory in 1958 to the medicine men they brought along with them to Sweden and who performed rituals in the locker room. But before the final in 1994, it was Italy that was hoping to benefit from the occult arts: "Black magic will prevent Brazil from winning," announced the Italian Union for Magic at the time—to no avail.

1998 // France

Sixty-four games, thirty-three days, and a record total of thirty-two teams. The 1998 World Cup in France was bigger and busier than ever before. For the first time it was also really big business for FIFA, which was able to take advantage of the earning opportunities provided by television and sponsors. But in doing so, it also angered many fans. Often, they were told that games had been sold out—only to discover later that many of the thousands of seats reserved for VIPs and sponsors remained empty. Even worse, the games were marred by terrible riots. Rowdy English hooligans marched through Marseille, and German hooligans left a path of destruction in the small town of Lens, beating a police officer half to death. Afterward, the German Football Association even briefly considered withdrawing from the World Cup. But as is usually the case with this sport, it was the fine game of soccer and the thrilling drama of the international competition that eventually prevailed—all those things that billions of people expect from the sport and ended up getting from the World Cup in France. However, it was the hosts themselves who received the richest reward. They valiantly fought their way up to their first World Cup title and were able to celebrate what midfielder Emmanuel Petit called the "greatest day since the French Revolution."

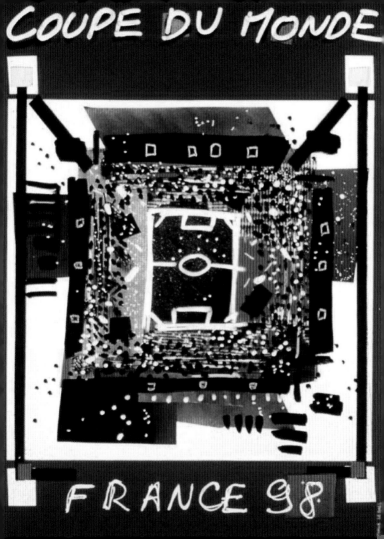

FIRST ROUND, GROUP A

Brazil vs. Scotland 2–1
Morocco vs. Norway 2–2
Scotland vs. Norway 1–1
Brazil vs. Morocco 3–0
Morocco vs. Scotland 3–0
Norway vs. Brazil 2–1

RESULTS
1. Brazil (Points: 6, Goals: 6–3)
2. Norway (5, 5–4)
3. Morocco (4, 5–5)
4. Scotland (1, 2–6)

FIRST ROUND, GROUP B

Italy vs. Chile 2–2
Cameroon vs. Austria 1–1
Chile vs. Austria 1–1
Italy vs. Cameroon 3–0
Italy vs. Austria 2–1
Chile vs. Cameroon 1–1

RESULTS
1. Italy (Points: 7, Goals: 7–3)
2. Chile (3, 4–4)
3. Austria (2, 3–4)
4. Cameroon (2, 2–5)

FIRST ROUND, GROUP C

Denmark vs. Saudi Arabia 1–0
France vs. South Africa 3–0
South Africa vs. Denmark 1–1
France vs. Saudi Arabia 4–0
France vs. Denmark 2–1
South Africa vs. Saudi Arabia 2–2

RESULTS
1. France (Points: 9, Goals: 9–1)
2. Denmark (4, 3–3)
3. South Africa (2, 3–6)
4. Saudi Arabia (1, 2–7)

FIRST ROUND, GROUP D

Paraguay vs. Bulgaria 0–0
Nigeria vs. Spain 3–2
Nigeria vs. Bulgaria 1–0
Paraguay vs. Spain 0–0
Spain vs. Bulgaria 6–1
Paraguay vs. Nigeria 3–1

RESULTS
1. Nigeria (Points: 6, Goals: 5–5)
2. Paraguay (5, 3–1)
3. Spain (4, 8–4)
4. Bulgaria (1, 1–7)

FIRST ROUND, GROUP E

Mexico vs. South Korea 3–1
Holland vs. Belgium 0–0
Belgium vs. Mexico 2–2
Holland vs. South Korea 5–0
Belgium vs. South Korea 1–1
Holland vs. Mexico 2–2

RESULTS
1. Holland (Points: 5, Goals: 7–2)
2. Mexico (5, 7–5)
3. Belgium (3, 3–3)
4. South Korea (1, 2–9)

FIRST ROUND, GROUP F

Yugoslavia vs. Iran 1–0
Germany vs. USA 2–0
Germany vs. Yugoslavia 2–2
Iran vs. USA 2–1
Germany vs. Iran 2–0
Yugoslavia vs. USA 1–0

RESULTS
1. Germany (Points: 7, Goals: 6–2)
2. Yugoslavia (7, 4–2)
3. Iran (3, 2–4)
4. USA (0, 1–5)

FIRST ROUND, GROUP G

England vs. Tunisia 2–0
Romania vs. Colombia 1–0
Colombia vs. Tunisia 1–0
Romania vs. England 2–1
Romania vs. Tunisia 1–1
England vs. Colombia 2–0

RESULTS

1. Romania (Points: 7, Goals: 4–2)
2. England (6, 5–2)
3. Colombia (3, 1–3)
4. Tunisia (1, 1–4)

FIRST ROUND, GROUP H

Argentina vs. Japan 1–0
Croatia vs. Jamaica 3–1
Croatia vs. Japan 1–0
Argentina vs. Jamaica 5–0
Jamaica vs. Japan 2–1
Argentina vs. Croatia 1–0

RESULTS

1. Argentina (Points: 9, Goals: 7–0)
2. Croatia (6, 4–2)
3. Jamaica (3, 3–9)
4. Japan (0, 1–4)

ROUND OF SIXTEEN

Italy vs. Norway 1–0
Brazil vs. Chile 4–1
France vs. Paraguay 1–0 OT
Denmark vs. Nigeria 4–1
Germany vs. Mexico 2–1
Holland vs. Yugoslavia 2–1
Croatia vs. Romania 1–0
Argentina vs. England 6–5 PEN

THIRD-PLACE MATCH

Croatia vs. Holland 2–1

QUARTERFINALS

France vs. Italy 4–3 PEN
Brazil vs. Denmark 3–2
Holland vs. Argentina 2–1
Croatia vs. Germany 3–0

SEMIFINALS

Brazil vs. Holland 5–3 PEN
France vs. Croatia 2–1

FINAL

France vs. Brazil 3–0

World Cup Champion: FRANCE

28 // October

North Africa against Northern Europe: the soccer compass was pointing south. Henning Berg lost the header duel against Said Chiba; Tore Andre Flo didn't get to the ball, but did tie up Youssef Rossi's shorts. With its quick combination play, Morocco's team simply was superior to the Norwegians. Despite this, the first surprise team of the World Cup was only able to secure a 2–2 draw: goalkeeper Driss Benzekri gave away the victory by committing two errors. In the end, the Norwegians were also thankful for their schedule: they didn't have to face Brazil until the last qualifying game. At that point the defending champion already had won the group after two victories against Scotland and Morocco and was able to slack off. Thanks to a controversial penalty kick, Norway went on to win 2–1 against Brazil, eliminating the powerless Moroccans from the tournament. ⚽

1998 // France

29 // October

> **Head and hand defense: Taribo West and his goalkeeper Peter Rufai clear a serious threat in the Nigerian penalty area.**

Standard situation: the whistle stops play due to a foul or the ball crossing the end line, and the referee awards either a corner or a free kick. The break only lasts a couple of seconds, and then the ball usually is kicked up high and far in front of the other team's goal—where leaping and heading ability is required. And that's exactly what the man with the most original hairdo in the 1998 World Cup could boast. Taribo West, the player with the green Rasta dreads, was able to get to the ball ahead of his goalkeeper and three Spanish attackers. Nigeria won this first qualifier 3–2, a loss which the Spanish team was never able to recover, despite a closing 6–1 win against Bulgaria. For decades, the Spaniards had been counted among the favorites, but once again they performed well below their potential and were eliminated in the qualifying round. ⚽

1998 // France

30 // October

Debutante ball: the red-and-white-checkered Croats and the green-and-yellow Jamaicans during both teams' first World Cup appearances ever. Like Zvonimir Boban in the jumping contest with Robbie Earle shown here, the Croats also dismissed the Jamaicans in the end and would make it big in the tournament. But despite their loss, the vibrant Caribbean players also were able to leave their mark. Their colorful attire and cheerful attitude made a valuable contribution to the atmosphere of the games in France. In particular, their 2–1 victory over Japan in the last game they played set off a small but lively Jamaican celebration. ⚽

31 // October

> Jürgen Klinsmann takes advantage of Tom Dooley's disorientation, shooting a goal for a 2–0 lead in the qualifier Germany vs. USA.

"**Hang down your head, Tom Dooley,** hang down your head and cry." Unlike his folk music namesake, Tom Dooley did not have to fear for his life after losing 0–2 against Germany. However, after the second goal—when Jürgen Klinsmann left him standing out in the cold after a trick and chest trap—the USA defender almost could have cried: "It happened in the most important game of my career. . . . I basically did everything wrong you could possibly do wrong," the American, who grew up in Germany, would say afterward. Later, Klinsmann and Dooley met up again in Southern California: Klinsmann settled there with his American wife, and Dooley started a youth soccer school. ⚽

1998 // France

1 // November

> The Nigerian Augustine "Jay Jay" Okocha doing a little ballroom dance with the Bulgarian players (from left) Trifon Ivanov, Ivailo Petkov, and Daniel Borimirov.

< Ball magician Augustine Okocha in the qualifying-round game Nigeria vs. Bulgaria 1–0.

....

....

....

....

Dribbling is what they call the pleasure of having the ball and keeping it. In modern-day soccer, with its emphasis on possessing the ball, short-pass games, and spacing, many coaches advise against dribbling: it's just too risky. That's why fans are all the happier when they see headstrong natural talents who refuse to let people stop them from doing something crazy with the ball—players like Augustine Okocha, better known as Jay Jay. In the German National Division in 1993 the Nigerian set a record in the unofficial category "suckering more opponents than necessary" when playing for Eintracht Frankfurt: he dribbled around so many Karlsruhe defenders that, in the end, he couldn't help but shoot a goal into a wide-open net. ⚽

2 // November

On June 21, 1998, Yugoslavia and Germany tied 2–2 in Lens—but different images were seen around the world on that day. They showed German hooligans on the rampage in the northern French town and almost beating a police officer, Daniel Nivel, to death. This despicable act exposed a gap in World Cup security measures: the stadiums themselves have long been safe, thanks to modern building techniques and surveillance systems. Violence there is virtually a thing of the past. However, outside of the arenas there is still plenty of opportunity for a handful of hooligans to stir up trouble before and after the games. Since the episode in Lens in 1998, the authorities have continued to work toward fixing these security gaps. ⚽

3 // November

> Austria's captain, Toni Polster (left), man-on-man with Paolo Maldini (Italy).

< Polster giving instruction to his teammates.

1998 // France

"Life punishes those who arrive too late": Mikhail Gorbachev's famous words on perestroika could also apply to Austria's soccer players a decade later. If there were an honorary title for achievements in individual phases of a game, Austria certainly would have been considered champion—world champions in the last minute, that is. Against Cameroon, for example, Toni Polster scored in the 90th minute for a 1–1 draw. Versus Chile, Ivica Vastic scored in the 90th minute, also 1–1. Against Italy, Andreas Herzog scored in the 90th minute—no, not for a 1–1 draw, but a 1–2 loss. This time the Austrians showed up too late. They were eliminated. ⚽

4 // November

Do gentlemen prefer blonds? We can only speculate whether Howard Hawks' film classic with Marilyn Monroe also inspired the Romanian team's new hairstyle. In any case, the team that had sported dark hair in its wins against Colombia and England went (almost) completely blond for the last qualifier against Tunisia. But just as in the biblical story of Samson, it seems that the players lost their strength when they lost their old hair-styles. After qualifying for the tournament and making it to the round of sixteen in a show of soccer skills superior to those of any of their European counterparts, the Romanians couldn't manage anything more than a 1–1 draw against Tunisia—and were finally elimi-nated with a 0–1 loss to Croatia. ⚽

5 // November

> Brazil's goalkeeper, Claudio Taffarel, grabs the ball away from Ivan Zamorano, the most dangerous Chilean on headers.
< The Brazilian Junior Baiano (left) frees the ball from Marcelo Salas (Chile) using his head.

As the Total Soccer of the Dutch inspired the world during the 1970s, a funny theory developed to explain how this free-flowing style of combination play may have come about. The Dutch invention could be traced back, or so the theory goes, to the tracts of low land the people of Holland had reclaimed from the sea. If you apply this theory to the geographical opposite of Holland—namely to Chile, that long, thin country squeezed between the Pacific and the Andes—it becomes clear that you can only really play soccer there if you launch balls very far and high. At least one player seemed to confirm this hypothesis: Ivan Zamorano, one of the most dangerous heading talents in the world. Although the forward had no chance against Brazil (1–4), the narrowest country in the world celebrated the second-best result of its history by reaching the round of sixteen—behind a third-place finish in what was essentially a home game in 1962. ⚽

6 // November

Norway's coach, Professor Egil Olsen, developed a soccer theory in the 1990s that led to some surprising victories for the small Scandinavian country. His research showed that having possession of the ball is not as important as the speed with which you get the ball you've just stolen to the opposing goal. According to Olsen, most goals are not scored after lengthy setup play or combination passes, but rather within seven seconds of winning the ball. With a game plan based on this theory, Norway even was able to defeat world-champion Brazil, though the Brazilians had won their group already. But, in the end, the round of sixteen was the final stop for the Scandinavians' rather simple game plan: the Italians had been familiar with this method for some time. ⚽

7 // November

....

....

....

....

....

He was the most dangerous goal-scoring threat among goalkeepers. In two decades as a professional, he shot sixty-three goals, eight of them while serving on Paraguay's national team. In fact, he was the first goalkeeper ever to manage a hat trick: three goals in a game. It's no surprise, then, that the opposing team's goalkeeper would start shaking at the knees when José Luis Chilavert deserted his box to take a penalty or free kick. But this was only one side of his talents. Named International Goalkeeper of the Year twice in his career, Chilavert was also an ace at defending his own goal. Thanks to his saves, Paraguay was able to eliminate Spain and Bulgaria from the tournament. But he was powerless against host France: in the 114th minute, Laurent Blanc scored the first Golden Goal in World Cup history against Chilavert. ⚽

8 // November

Music, please! Painted and clad in green and white, the Nigerian fans could do little more than watch in horror as their star team's performance quickly went out of tune. Four years earlier, Africa's strongest team played exceedingly well, losing to Italy only because of some reckless mistakes. But this time they completely fell apart in the round of sixteen. When the Laudrup brothers joined forces to produce a 4–1 win for Denmark, the African soccer fans were forced to come to a bitter realization: the revolution in African soccer heralded by Cameroon's stellar performance in 1990 had failed to materialize. Characterized by simple enjoyment of the game, athletic power, and complete disorganization, the Africans were no match for the Europeans or South Americans.

9 // November

> England's 1998 World Cup star: the 18-year-old Liverpool player Michael Owen.

< David Seaman, England's premier goalkeeper.

Chasing a place in World Cup history: Michael Owen collected the ball in his own half of the field and went right to the goal—with Jose Chamot trying to take him down. But accelerating like a rocket, he left Chamot, and then Roberto Ayala, in the dust, shooting the ball over goalkeeper Carlos Roa from eighteen yards out. This winning goal against Argentina 2–1 gave England a new national hero, an eighteen-year-old lad from Liverpool; many were celebrating him already as the best thing from Liverpool since the Beatles.

10 // November

While Michael Owen was celebrated as a hero, David Beckham was the Brits' worst nightmare at his first World Cup. With the score tied at 2–2 in the heated duel against Argentina, Beckham kicked out at Argentinean midfielder Diego Simeone after being tackled from behind only moments earlier. Even though the kick was hardly painful, Simeone played it up, falling theatrically to the ground. (Years later he would admit that it was just a performance.) But Beckham was shown the red card, and the devastated English team ended up losing on penalty kicks following overtime. The English papers showed no mercy, running the headline: "Ten brave lions and one stupid boy." Not until three years later, when he shot England into the 2002 World Cup with one of his brilliant free kicks in the last minute against Greece, did his countrymen forgive the pop star of soccer.

11 // November

Gymnastics lesson for soccer players: the German Michael Tarnat bends; the Croatian Mario Stanic flies over him as if leapfrogging, but lands hard. Oliver Bierhoff looks on, clearly impressed. But, as witnessed during the entire ninety minutes of the quarterfinal game, it was the Germans who hardly could find their footing. ⚽

Two German trumps that didn't trump: in the twenty-fifth and last World Cup game of his career, Lothar Matthäus (right) made a crucial positioning mistake against Croatian Davor Suker, which forced Christian Wörns to tangle with the star striker. A red card was the result. Playing short, Germany battled on in vain. And Oliver Bierhoff, the goal scoring king of the Italian Serie A feared as the best forward in the world at heading the ball, didn't get any decent chances for headers. The Croatian coach, Miroslav Blazevic, explained his team's win with a military comparison: just as the Allies once defeated the German Rommel in North Africa by cutting off his fuel supplies, Blazevic's troops "deprived Klinsmann and Bierhoff of the ball." ⚽

13 // November

The soccer field is normally more than 6,400 square yards in size. Yet here, Edgar Davids and Emerson have laid claim to the very same square foot of the pitch—visual proof of the incredible determination of the Dutch and Brazilian teams as they battle in perhaps the best World Cup game of the 1990s for a spot in the final.

1998 // France

14 // November

The color yellow dominates the length of the Brazilian goal—but orange controls the airspace around it: Patrick Kluivert with a header. Shortly before the end of the fantastic second half, the striker scored a well-deserved equalizer for the Dutchmen, who had put all of their playing magic into combating the Brazilians and their outstanding scorer, Ronaldo. In overtime, both sides failed to convert the Golden Goal that would have ended the match. Kluivert's shot was the closest. But then it came down to the worst punishment of all for Holland: a penalty shootout.

15 // November

The goalkeeper's helplessness during the penalty kick: in the semifinal between Brazil and the Dutch, Edwin van der Sar only conceded one goal to Ronaldo, which Patrick Kluivert was able to equalize later. But during the penalty shootout, van der Sar didn't stand a chance. Just as in the European Championships in 1992, 1996, and 2000, the Dutch lost this World Cup on penalties—and this despite having their best team since the Cruyff era.

16 // November

> The Brazilians celebrate their goalkeeper
Claudio Taffarel, without whom they wouldn't
have made it to the final.

In a country like Brazil, the scorers are almost always the stars, not the goalkeepers. But that all changes when it comes to a penalty shootout: a goalkeeper who can stop a shot becomes a celebrated man, even in the country of the most talented goal scorers. This is precisely what Claudio Taffarel was able to do, successfully blocking penalty kicks by Dutchmen Philip Cocu and Ronald de Boer, thus taking Brazil to the final. Here, Taffarel is almost suffocated by his adoring teammates.

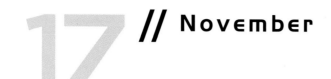

17 // November

Campfire for fans in the guest section: at the halftime whistle, Croatian backers rejoiced over their lead on Davor Suker's goal. For the first time in the tournament, the World Cup host, France, was trailing its opponent. But two goals by defender Lilian Thuram would turn the match around for the French, who moved on to the final against Brazil with a 2–1 win. ⚽

1998 // France

18 // November

> Davor Suker has every reason to be proud of himself and his team after their win over the Dutch.

< Suker in the semifinal against France.

....

....

....

....

Goal scorer, flag bearer. Here, Davor Suker is not only celebrating his team's third-place World Cup finish, secured with a 2–1 win over Holland, but also the imaginary top-scorer crown he has earned by shooting six World Cup goals. ⚽

1998 // France

19 // November

Soccer, a video game: the enormous display screen in the Stade de France in Saint-Denis (outside Paris) shows the equivalent of a dream final. Brazil versus France, July 12, 1998—that's two days before France's official national holiday. However, as fate would have it, the French would celebrate their holiday two days early this year. ⚽

> Zinedine Zidane heads the ball into the Brazilians' net to lead 1–0.

< A 2–0 shot by Zidane, once again with his head.

The key player and passer in midfield is usually referred to as the head of the team. In the final against the Brazilians, Zinedine Zidane proved that the head of the team can take his title literally. In doing so, he surprised the Brazilians, who weren't familiar with this side of the French ball artist. After a corner kick, Zidane jumped up and, in midair, shot a front header, netting the leading goal. Shortly afterwards in the 45th minute, Zidane put another header past the Brazilian goalkeeper—but this time from the other side, and almost from a standing position. He was completely unmarked at the time. The Brazilians trailed France by two goals for the rest of the game—until the last minute, when Emmanuel Petit scored the final goal for a 3–0 victory. ⚽

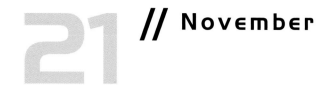

21 // November

Zinedine I, Soccer King of France: the playmaker and two-time scorer presents himself to his adoring fans. And this even though Zidane had to sit out a good portion of this World Cup and could only keep his fingers crossed for his teammates. If they hadn't won the games against Paraguay (with Laurent Blanc's Golden Goal) and against Italy (on penalties), Zidane would have become his country's whipping boy, just like David Beckham after his red card in the game against Argentina. Why? In the qualifier against Saudi Arabia, Zidane committed a payback foul and was banned from playing in the next three games. His teammates survived without him, preparing the stage for the son of Algerian immigrants to become the new French national hero. ⚽

> In his only remarkable play of the contest, Ronaldo can't get to the ball ahead of goalkeeper Fabien Barthez, who's diving at neck-breaking speed.

< Keeping a cool head: Fabien Barthez.

Where was Ronaldo, anyway? The behavior of the man who, until the final, had been the best player of the World Cup remains a mystery. To start with, the Brazilian didn't even show up for the warm-up in the stadium. Then rumors spread that Ronaldo had collapsed and been sent to the hospital. In the end, he showed up—but only as a shadow of his former self. To this very day, the mystery of his odd behavior has not been fully solved. He even had to explain his team's loss to a parliamentary committee appointed to combat corruption in Brazilian soccer. "Why didn't we win?" asked Ronaldo, repeating the question asked by one member of parliament. "Because we allowed three goals. Because we lost," he answered. If only all political investigations could be so simple!

France was the first world champion to have players from five continents on its roster (Africa, South America, Asia, Oceania, and Europe). Three had roots in sub-Saharan Africa (Marcel Desailly, Lilian Thuram, and Patrick Vieira), one in northern Africa (Zinedine Zidane), two in South America (David Trezeguet and Bernard Lama), one in the Caribbean (Thierry Henry), one in Asia (Youri Djorkaeff), and one in Oceania (Christian Karembeu). Together with the European players Didier Deschamps, Emmanuel Petit, and Laurent Blanc, they formed a global team with a single national identity. The country saw a reflection of French society and culture in the diversity of the talented players. The philosopher Alain Finkielkraut stated: "Even beyond the soccer field, our victory is one of hospitality and diverse descent."

24 // November

Even the victory arch was glowing. On July 12, 1998, France celebrated "the greatest day since the French Revolution" (Emmanuel Petit). But it wasn't a holiday for everybody. Because defenders and midfielders had scored all French goals since the World Cup qualifying round, somebody came up with the mean-spirited saying that France was the first country to become world champion without any strikers. Naturally, this especially upset the only French forward in the final game, Stéphane Guivarc'h. Twice he was open; twice he failed miserably—just like he had failed to score throughout the entire World Cup. And to add insult to injury, the bag with his world champion jersey and the jersey of his opponent, Junior Baiano, was stolen. Thus, the day may have belonged to almost sixty million French people—but it didn't belong to Stéphane Guivarc'h. ⚽

2002 // South Korea & Japan

The first World Cup to be held in two different countries led to many complications in planning—like the question of who would organize and host the final (Japan), and which country's name would appear first in the official title of the event (South Korea). However, good organization and the gleam of the new stadiums overshadowed all of this. The mood was often dampened by weak performances by referees—Portugal, Italy, and Spain were eliminated due to bad calls, all of which benefited host South Korea. In addition, many of the world's best—all of whom played on European teams—were injured or run down, including Zinedine Zidane, Luis Figo, and David Beckham. This was mainly due to the Champions League, which had demanded more and more of the players' time and energy since the mid-1990s. Despite these shortcomings—and the unusual game times, for European viewers, where the kickoff for most matches took place in the morning—the World Cup bug managed to spread across the globe. In fact, many European countries came to a virtual standstill while workers cheered on their teams, often in bars or at public squares on large viewing screens. It was a new type of social gathering, and an entirely new World Cup feel: a time-out right in the middle of the workday.

© 1999 FIFA TM

2002
FIFA WORLD CUP
KOREA JAPAN

FIRST ROUND, GROUP A

Senegal vs. France 1–0
Denmark vs. Uruguay 2–1
Senegal vs. Denmark 1–1
France vs. Uruguay 0–0
Denmark vs. France 2–0
Senegal vs. Uruguay 3–3

RESULTS
1. Denmark (Points: 7, Goals: 5–2)
2. Senegal (5, 5–4)
3. Uruguay (2, 4–5)
4. France (1, 0–3)

FIRST ROUND, GROUP B

Paraguay vs. South Africa 2–2
Spain vs. Slovenia 3–1
Spain vs. Paraguay 3–1
South Africa vs. Slovenia 1–0
Spain vs. South Africa 3–2
Paraguay vs. Slovenia 3–1

RESULTS
1. Spain (Points: 9, Goals: 9–4)
2. Paraguay (4, 6–6)
3. South Africa (4, 5–5)
4. Slovenia (0, 2–7)

FIRST ROUND, GROUP C

Brazil vs. Turkey 2–1
Costa Rica vs. China 2–0
Brazil vs. China 4–0
Costa Rica vs. Turkey 1–1
Brazil vs. Costa Rica 5–2
Turkey vs. China 3–0

RESULTS
1. Brazil (Points: 9, Goals: 11–3)
2. Turkey (4, 5–3)
3. Costa Rica (4, 5–6)
4. China (0, 0–9)

FIRST ROUND, GROUP D

South Korea vs. Poland 2–0
USA vs. Portugal 3–2
South Korea vs. USA 1–1
Portugal vs. Poland 4–0
South Korea vs. Portugal 1–0
Poland vs. USA 3–1

RESULTS
1. South Korea (Points: 7, Goals: 4–1)
2. USA (4, 5–6)
3. Portugal (3, 6–4)
4. Poland (3, 3–7)

FIRST ROUND, GROUP E

Ireland vs. Cameroon 1–1
Germany vs. Saudi Arabia 8–0
Germany vs. Ireland 1–1
Cameroon vs. Saudi Arabia 1–0
Germany vs. Cameroon 2–0
Ireland vs. Saudi Arabia 3–0

RESULTS
1. Germany (Points: 7, Goals: 11–1)
2. Ireland (5, 5–2)
3. Cameroon (4, 2–3)
4. Saudi Arabia (: 0, 0–12)

FIRST ROUND, GROUP F

Argentina vs. Nigeria 1–0
England vs. Sweden 1–1
Sweden vs. Nigeria 2–1
England vs. Argentina 1–0
Sweden vs. Argentina 1–1
Nigeria vs. England 0–0

RESULTS
1. Sweden (Points: 5, Goals: 4–3)
2. England (5, 2–1)
3. Argentina (4, 2–2)
4. Nigeria (1, 1–3)

FIRST ROUND, GROUP G

Mexico vs. Croatia 1–0
Italy vs. Ecuador 2–0
Croatia vs. Italy 2–1
Mexico vs. Ecuador 2–1
Mexico vs. Italy 1–1
Ecuador vs. Croatia 1–0

RESULTS

1. Mexico (Points: 7, Goals: 4–2)
2. Italy (4, 4–3)
3. Croatia 3, 2–3)
4. Ecuador (3, 2–4)

FIRST ROUND, GROUP H

Japan vs. Belgium 2–2
Russia vs. Tunisia 2–0
Japan vs. Russia 1–0
Tunisia vs. Belgium 1–1
Japan vs. Tunisia 2–0
Belgium vs. Russia 3–2

RESULTS

1. Japan (Points: 7, Goals: 5–2)
2. Belgium (5, 6–5)
3. Russia (3, 4–4)
4. Tunisia (1, 1–5)

ROUND OF SIXTEEN

Germany vs. Paraguay 1–0
England vs. Denmark 3–0
Senegal vs. Sweden 2–1 OT
Spain vs. Ireland 4–3 PEN
USA vs. Mexico 2–0
Brazil vs. Belgium 2–0
Turkey vs. Japan 1–0
South Korea vs. Italy 2–1 OT

THIRD-PLACE MATCH

Turkey vs. South Korea 3–2

QUARTERFINALS

Brazil vs. England 2–1
Germany vs. USA 1–0
South Korea vs. Spain 5–3 PEN
Turkey vs. Senegal 1–0 OT

SEMIFINALS

Germany vs. South Korea 1–0
Brazil vs. Turkey 1–0

FINAL

Brazil vs. Germany 2–0

World Cup Champion: BRAZIL

27 // November

Soccer stadiums are often called modern-day temples. But even if you consider talk about soccer having a pseudoreligious function to be nonsense, it can't be denied that the soccer boom that started in the 1990s has produced numerous examples of amazing stadium architecture throughout the world. Most of the twenty stadiums used in the 2002 World Cup in South Korea and Japan were built especially for the occasion, including the World Cup Stadium in Seoul, where the opening ceremony and the opening game took place. With a capacity of sixty-five thousand spectators, it is the largest stadium in all of Asia. ⚽

28 // November

A tray as an international stage: South Korea celebrated the opening of the World Cup with a myriad of colors, forms, and flawless mass choreography. Many visitors felt that the Seoul World Cup Stadium was one of the most beautiful soccer arenas in the world. Its basic structure is based on the *soban,* a traditional octagonal tea tray made of wood. Other elements of Korean tradition also are visible in the stadium's design. The roof, for example, combines the shape of a sailing ship on the Han River with that of a traditional Korean kite that is said to carry the hopes of humanity to heaven. During this World Cup, the dragon really did end up taking the Koreans' soccer hopes to unexpectedly great heights.

29 // November

Numbers lie, even in soccer. Before the 2002 World Cup, the magazine *France Football* had calculated that, with only 8 losses in the last 101 national games, France's team was "the most difficult team to beat in the history of soccer." Moreover, none of the losses was by more than one goal. A historical comparison shows that only Hungary's Wonder Team, between 1945 and 1956, had achieved a result comparable to that of the Equipe Tricolore between 1994 and May 31, 2002—the evening of the World Cup opening game against Senegal. No wonder most experts considered the defending champion the favorite, even if France's injured star, Zinedine Zidane, wasn't able to participate in the match against Senegal. But in the end, everything turned out quite different from people's expectations. ⚽

30 // November

> **False start in the opening game: the Frenchman Sylvain Wiltord jumps between Omar Daf (left) and Papa Bouba Diop, but to no avail. Diop goes on to score the winning goal.**

Brought back down to earth with a bump—that's what happened to France in the 2002 World Cup. The French players, who no longer played for professional teams in France, but rather elsewhere for the best European clubs, suffered a rude awakening in their opening game against Senegal. Interestingly, most of the players on the Senegalese team played at the time for clubs in France—one of the many odd twists in the global soccer business.

Soccer ballet with Swan Lake: the Big Swan Stadium in the Japanese city of Niigata was one of the spectacular new stadiums of the 2002 World Cup. It stood out with its translucent-white Teflon roof, whose rolling shape was designed to call to mind the swans on the adjacent lagoon.

2 // December

It's possible to lose a World Cup before the tournament even starts. Thanks to some poor travel planning, Cameroon's team and its German coach, Winfried Schäfer, were subjected to a marathon journey before they finally arrived in Japan six days late. Their circuitous route had taken them to Paris, Ethiopia, India, and Thailand along the way. In addition, they had problems with FIFA, which prohibited Cameroon from wearing the tight-fitting, sleeveless one-piece uniforms the team had so successfully sported during the African championship. The Irish, on the other hand, had lost their captain and best player, Roy Keane, who was sent home after insulting coach Mick McCarthy. The two weakened group opponents parted with a 1–1 draw—and hardly figured in the rest of the tournament.

> Team photo of the Chinese national team.

< A big little fan from China.

The game always needs new markets, so China was a closely watched newcomer to the World Cup. In the 1990s, the country with the largest population in the world discovered its enthusiasm for the most popular game in the world. But it's a big step from being an economic power to becoming a soccer success. Even coach Bora Milutinovic couldn't prevent the Chinese disappointment. The Serb, one of the biggest travelers in international soccer, reached the round of sixteen in four different World Cup tournaments between 1986 and 1998 with four different teams: Mexico, Costa Rica, USA, and Nigeria. But this time he was powerless. The Chinese were eliminated in their first World Cup with zero points and a combined 0–9 score in three games.

4 // December

Red is an appropriate color for the land of the rising sun: while the Belgian soccer players call themselves Red Devils and dress accordingly, the Japanese Kazuyuki Toda got himself a matching hairdo before the game. Belgium and Japan parted 2–2. Both survived their qualifying group, but Belgium went on to lose miserably in the round of sixteen to Brazil, and Japan lost by a narrow margin to Turkey. All that was left for them to do was see red. ⚽

5 // December

> Even gods of the goal are fallible: Robbie Keane was the only shooter to overpower German goalkeeper Oliver Kahn before the final.

Cerberus is an old-fashioned nickname for goalkeepers—after the dog that guarded the entrance to the underworld in Greek mythology. And just as the ferocious Cerberus guarded the gate to Hades, so did Oliver Kahn protect the goal of the German national team. Only a single opposing player was able to overwhelm him during the first six games of the World Cup: the Irishman Robbie Keane, who scored an equalizer (1–1) in the qualifying round. Indeed, Kahn was the first goalkeeper to reach a World Cup final having conceded only one goal. Before the final, he became the first goalie to be selected as the best player of the World Cup. "Titan" and "goalkeeper god" were some of the words used to describe him in the press. But then came the final. And the goalie god became a mortal once again.

6 // December

> Patrick Vieira (France) getting physical with Uruguay's goalkeeper Fabian Carini (left photo). On the right, the Mexican referee Felipe Ramos Rizo, who is clearly in a better mood than Sylvain Wiltord (France, right) or Marcelo Romero (Uruguay, left).

It doesn't matter how you get to the World Cup: in the end you often end up with the same result. France had the shortest route of all in 2002. As defending champions, the French automatically qualified (and, incidentally, were the last to have this privilege, because now the most recent world champion also has to make it through the maze of continental qualification). Uruguay, on the other hand, had contested the eighteen matches of the South American group and then, after failing to qualify with a fifth-place finish, still had to endure two games against Australia, the winner of the Oceania zone. The one country didn't need any play to qualify, but the other had to go through twenty games. In the end, they parted 0-0. ⚽

7 // December

> David Beckham (left) converted the deciding penalty kick against Argentina after a foul on Michael Owen (right).

< English fans, well-equipped with flags.

You should not always listen to your wife: David Beckham's wife had told him not to shoot a penalty kick in the heated duel against the World Cup favorites Argentina, with whom England had had a special rivalry since the Falklands War and two World Cup losses in 1986 and 1998. But then the great Michael Owen was fouled, and the captain ignored the advice of Victoria Beckham: he stepped up to the penalty spot and hammered the ball into the net. Back home in England, where the game was being broadcast in the morning hours, twenty percent of the workforce had taken the day off, seventy percent of those at work were watching on the job, and most others had called in sick. There was an explosion of national exuberance after England, with its 1–0 victory, ended Argentina's eighteen-game winning streak. "The most momentous victory at a World Cup since 1966," hailed the *Daily Telegraph,* referring to England's 1966 World Cup win. ⚽

8 // December

Off to battle, matador: Fernando Morientes, swinging his national jersey like a red cape, is celebrated like a great bullfighter by his teammates Fernando Hierro and Carlos Puyol. With its 3–1 win against Paraguay, the Spaniards advanced early to the round of sixteen and celebrated their best World Cup start in decades. ⚽

9 // December

As sunny as the Azores: in this image, Portuguese fans are celebrating the 4–0 victory over Poland, a sign that Portugal had overcome the opening 2–3 defeat at the hands of the United States. Three of these goals were shot by striker Pedro Pauleta—the first Portuguese national team player to come from the Azores. But in the last group-stage encounter, Portugal was in for a stormy ride. Battling against host South Korea, the team suffered the same fate Italy and Spain would later: the referee disallowed a perfectly good goal and the Portuguese were eliminated 0–1.

> One person's joy is another's sorrow: a Danish and a French fan, following the reigning champion's unexpectedly swift elimination from the tournament at the hands of the Scandinavians.
< Jon Dahl Tomasson (Denmark), who shot the winning second goal against France 2–0.

Goodbye France, bonjour tristesse: to its fans' dismay, France flunks what would be its final test in the World Cup by losing 0–2 to Denmark, thus becoming the first reigning champion in World Cup history to be eliminated during the preliminary round—without even scoring a single goal. Back in northern Europe, the soccer-go-lucky Danes witnessed how their triumph proved infectious, spreading even beyond their borders: "Almost two hundred years after the Danish-Norwegian union, jubilation has spread from the Jutland peninsula to the Oslofjord," the newspaper *VG* reported. The following morning, the Swedes joined the pan-Scandinavian chorus when their team eliminated Argentina with a 1–1 draw. Instead of the odds-on favorites France and Argentina, the underdog Scandinavians pulled into the next round. Copenhagen went wild, and in Stockholm the fans gathered in the famous Sergels Torg and took a dip in the fountain. ⚽

> **Michael Owen and Efetobore Sodje during the group encounter between England and Nigeria 0–0.**
< **England's Michael Owen.**

Soccer, a game with telepathic powers. For the second time, the World Cup in East Asia brought public life in far distant England to a standstill. As during the triumph against Argentina, a whole country absconded from the morning shift to see its red-clad heroes in action. Twenty-five thousand pubs opened at 7 a.m., schools postponed the day's first classes, and factories like Nissan in Sunderland stopped the conveyor belts—the backlog of 190 vehicles had to be dealt with by the round of sixteen. London rush hour was postponed until after the final whistle at 9:20, English time. In the end, a 0–0 draw against Nigeria was all that was needed to move on, and the event turned out to be exactly what national coach Sven-Göran Eriksson predicted from the Far East: "A nice, quiet breakfast for the fans back home." ⚽

12 // December

The sickle-shaped curve of the main grandstand seems to intertwine almost tenderly with its smaller counterpart on the opposite side of the Miyagi Stadium in Sendai. Here, too, the Japanese remained loyal to their architectural tradition of combining modern technology with natural and historic elements. The sickle form of the main grandstand is reminiscent of the headpiece on the helmets worn by local warriors during the feudal period. But the Japanese were unable to live up to their ancestors' fighting spirit: they were eliminated in the Miyagi Stadium after a 0–1 defeat to Turkey in the round of sixteen. ⚽

13 // December

> Henrik Larsson (Sweden) with a free kick in front of the Argentinean wall.

< Swedish soccer and makeup fan.

A truly masterful free kick combines the action of both the hammer and sickle, as Henrik Larsson demonstrated, putting spin on the ball as he shot full force, curving it around the Argentinean wall but narrowly missing the goal. In the end, though, a 1–1 draw against Argentina was enough for the Scandinavians to topple the two-time world champions in the qualifying round.

14 // December

When Ahn Jung-Hwan missed a penalty kick in the game against Italy in the round of sixteen, no one would have believed that he would become Korea's soccer hero after the game was over. But in overtime, he scored the Golden Goal with a header, which ended the game and meant a sensational victory for the host over the three-time world champions (in a sudden-death overtime, the first goal scored immediately ends the match; thus its nickname, the Golden Goal). The Italians quarreled with the referee, and rightly so: he had disallowed a legitimate goal and sent star Francesco Totti from the pitch. As revenge for the Korean star having eliminated Italy, the fans wanted to kick Ahn Jung-Hwan off the Italian club he played with—AC Perugia. Luckily, it didn't come to this. And in Korea, on this evening, Ahn became an eternal hero. Millions of fans poured into the streets to celebrate his goal. ⚽

15 // December

> Brad Friedel, the first goalkeeper in World Cup history to block two penalty kicks during normal playing time (against South Korea and Poland), here keeps a clean sheet against the Mexican Luis Hernandez, with the help of Eddie Pope (left).
< Claudio Reyna celebrates the 2–0 victory over Mexico.

Are players true to their names? Sometimes. In any case, a glance at the lineup in the World Cup round of sixteen would lead anyone with a bit of superstition and the right literary background to guess that Mexico was at a disadvantage against the United States. A player by the name of Pope was in the U.S. team's defense, while the literary allusion in the names of numbers 2, 3, and 4 on the Mexican team was perhaps not quite as obvious: their names were Gabriel, Garcia, Marquez. Unfortunately, even if a name like this can win you a Nobel prize in literature, it can't win you a World Cup, too. ⚽

16 // December

A picture that makes shampoo manufacturers shudder. Kieron Dyer and Stig Töfting aren't the only ones to make a clear cut of it: the buzz cut is a popular style among professional soccer players. The world of soccer fashion has witnessed many disastrous hairstyles, but there's no risk with a nicely polished shaved head. At the 1998 World Cup, defense leader Laurent Blanc's smacker on goalkeeper Fabien Barthez's head became a Gallic victory ritual. At the other extreme, who can forget the shaggy haircuts of the Argentineans, the frizzy hair of Spain's players, or the Japanese with their blazing dyed locks? But it was the top scorer Ronaldo who found the perfect balance: he shaved his head, but left a postcard-sized patch of hair at the front. ⚽

17 // December

Soccer, an encounter in the third dimension: fans often complain about a lack of dynamics and how the game has become too centered around horizontal play, especially when passes are deep in the other team's half. But the ball almost always goes up in the air, too. Here, the Spaniard Fernando Morientes plays one flight up against the Irishman Matt Holland, just like the German Thomas Linke against the American Landon Donovan. ⚽

In Ireland, three sectors in particular profit from the World Cup: pubs, banks, and travel agencies. Just like in 1990 on the way to the quarterfinal, in Italy in 2002 many fans booked World Cup trips with their credit cards. And whoever couldn't afford (or didn't want to pay for) the trips racked up a fine bill at the pub, where the games were broadcast in the early hours of the morning. After the 2–0 victory over Saudi Arabia, which secured the Irish a spot in the round of sixteen after draws in the games against Cameroon and Germany, the "longest lunch break in Irish history" (according to the BBC) was celebrated at dawn. The celebration continued for 120 minutes against Spain—and ended with a shootout. Three Irish players missed. But the Spaniards Fernando Hierro (shown here) and then Gaizka Mendieta scored—and thus began what was perhaps the worst hangover in Irish history. ⚽

19 // December

> Michael Ballack (Germany) applauds the fans after Germany's victory over Paraguay in the round of sixteen.

< The Jeju World Cup Stadium on the South Korean island of Cheju.

Soccer with a view. Nestled on top of Gogunsan mountain on the island of Cheju, a popular vacation destination, the Jeju World Cup Stadium doesn't have to fear comparisons with any other soccer stadium. With its fiberglass roof suspended by steel cables, it is reminiscent of a sail blown full by a stormy wind, thus mirroring the tradition and beauty of the island. At least for the German team and its followers, it opened up a view that stretched out wide over the sea as far as Japan: with their 1–0 victory over Paraguay, Rudi Völler's team took a giant step in the direction of the championship final in Yokohama.

> There's no way that Paraguayan Roque Santa
Cruz is going to get around the German defender
Thomas Linke (left).
< Sebastian Kehl (left) in a header duel with Jose
Cardozo in the game between Germany and
Paraguay 1–0 in the round of sixteen.

Career Bavarians in their ranks: Thomas Linke, from Thuringia in the eastern part of Germany, man-on-man with the Paraguayan Roque Santa Cruz—both players for FC Bayern Munich. Linke was one of the most solid defenders in the World Cup and, together with center back Christoph Metzelder and goalkeeper Oliver Kahn, who conceded only one goal in six games, laid the foundation for Germany's progression to the championship final. Paraguay had the meager consolation of being entered into the book of World Cup records: the team's coach, Cesare Maldini, was the oldest in World Cup history. The Italian, father of the record-breaking national player Paolo Maldini, was seventy years old at the time. ⚽

21 // December

Like one of those newfangled energy drinks, soccer can give you wings—but it took a while before Brazil's soccer artists were able to glean inspiration from the architecture of the Kobe Wing Stadium. In their game against Belgium in the round of sixteen, they needed the referee to spot them; he disallowed a perfectly legitimate goal shot by Marc Wilmots, which would have put Belgium in the lead. In the end, Brazil achieved a win with goals by stars Rivaldo and Ronaldo. ⚽

2002 // **South Korea & Japan**

22 // December

> England's striker Michael Owen (left), who shot the goal for a 1–0 lead over Brazil, here man-on-man with Lucio (Brazil).
< Disappointed: David Beckham (England) after the final whistle.

The ball soars, and with it the hearts of millions: Michael Owen lifted the ball over goalkeeper Marcos and scored in the first half against Brazil. But David Beckham's delay just before halftime in the middle of a one-on-one with Ronaldinho gave Brazil an opportunity to equalize. And in the second half, a blunder by goalkeeper David Seaman during a free kick by Ronaldinho robbed England of its chance of victory. Here (photo left), captain Beckham leaves the field with a Brazilian jersey on his shoulders, the captain's band in hand, and tears in his eyes. Once again, no success: England's World Cup losing streak of forty years continued. ⚽

23 // December

> Ronaldinho twice: in the qualifier against Turkey (left) and in the quarterfinal against England.

Dancing with the ball: in the qualifier, Ronaldinho leaves a Turkish player behind, and celebrates his free kick against England in the quarterfinal. Despite all his skill with the ball, he remained the Little Ronaldo, a result of the somewhat silly system of stage names for Brazilian soccer players. In the mid-1990s, there were two Ronaldos already: a goalkeeper and a defender. To differentiate between them, the defender was called Ronaldao (big Ronaldo). Then along came today's Ronaldo, who was named Ronaldinho (little Ronaldo). In 1999, yet another Ronaldo came along, whom we today know as Ronaldinho— but at that time, he couldn't be called Ronaldinho, because there was another Ronaldinho already. As a result, he was called Ronaldinho Gaucho (after his home state of Rio Grande do Sul). Later, both were promoted: Ronaldinho became Ronaldo and Ronaldinho Gaucho became Ronaldinho. ⚽

24 // December

The card that cost him the dream of his career: every player dreams of standing on the field in a championship final at least once in his life. In the semifinal game between Germany and South Korea, Michael Ballack committed a tactical foul, causing Lee to fall to the ground and thus denying him a shot at the goal. Ballack could guess already what disaster referee Urs Meier would pull from his pocket: the yellow card. As his second yellow card, it meant a suspension. Such a fate had befallen others already: the Englishman Paul Gascoigne in 1990 against Germany, who broke into tears over it; and the Italian Alessandro Costacurta in 1994, when he had to sit out the final game in the Champions League with Milan, as well as the World Cup final game with Italy. But no one reacted quite like Ballack. "The guy gets a booking. He's going to miss the final whatever. Does he burst into tears, does he lose his head? No, he goes up the other end and scores the winner for them," reported London's *Times*. ⚽

25 // December

> Rivaldo man-on-man with Emre Belözoglu in the semifinal Brazil vs. Turkey 1–0.
< Emre Belözoglu is beat after the semifinal, which Turkey lost.

In the preliminary game against Turkey, Rivaldo gave his team a leg up with his head. Out of anger over a free-kick call, the Turk Hakan Ünsal shot the ball at Rivaldo's leg. However, Rivaldo immediately covered his face with his hands as if the ball had hit his face, and thus Ünsal was given a red card. In their second encounter, this time in the semifinal, Rivaldo really used his noggin and didn't depend solely on his acting talent.

26 // December

Greetings from Tokyo! The Turkish team waves to their friends back home after their 3–2 win against South Korea in the game for third place, in which Hakan Sükür shot the fastest goal in World Cup history, after only ten seconds. "Now we're going to celebrate with our fans," promised coach Senol Günes. "They love this team, and the players love their fans. Our reception at home will be an encounter between lovers."

2002 // South Korea & Japan

27 // December

In 1998, Germany's neighbors in Europe were rightly able to gloat over the performance of the country that is typically seen as the model child of soccer. Following Germany's 0–3 loss to Croatia, the French *Journal du Dimanche* wrote: "The eternal sweepers are going home." But four years later, the sweepers won again, as if the World Cup flops of 1994 and 1998 had never happened. Nevertheless, in this seventh final game in the history of German soccer, the Germans had never been so dull, spreading disillusionment throughout the world. The English *Sun* praised "through clenched teeth . . . the unaccountable quality of the Germans, their mental strength." The French *Parisian* saw a team "that remained true to its tradition, without genius, without pity, devilishly solid and realistic." And the Swiss *Neue Zürcher Zeitung* described a performance without equal in World Cup history: "To pull into the championship final after such an easy series of games without having once played an utterly convincing game."

28 // December

> Ballet on the pitch: the German Dietmar Hamann (middle, below) against Rivaldo (right) and his teammates.

< Rivaldo (middle) brings some excitement into the German penalty area.

Brazil vs. Germany—a logical, yet entirely crazy, finale. It was strange enough that the two most successful countries in World Cup history had never played each other in a championship final. But it was even stranger that they would meet in this World Cup, of all tournaments—and in the final game to boot: their performances in the qualifying rounds had been weaker than at any point in their previous fifty years, and both were considered underdogs. But these factoids are odd only if you look at things from a short-term perspective. Seen from the long term, it was the logical conclusion for twentieth-century soccer: Brazil with its four World titles pitted against Germany with three. Ever since the end of World War II, with the exception of 1978, one of these two teams had been in the championship final. Now, for the first time, both of them were. It was as if this World Cup served to decide the champion of the entire twentieth century, albeit two years late. ⚽

> So close, yet so far: the German goalkeeper Oliver Kahn can't stop Ronaldo's goal, which puts Brazil up 1–0.

< Oliver Kahn and national coach Michael Skibbe (left) still have to come to terms with their defeat.

....

....

....

....

....

The first mistake was one mistake too many. The danger, indeed the special tragedy, that can befall the goalkeeper, the last man between the ball and the net—even Oliver Kahn was not immune to it. No other goalkeeper had dominated a World Cup tournament quite as he had: with numerous magnificent saves, he conceded only one goal in six games. Yet no goalkeeper lost a World Cup final quite like him either—with a single embarrassing slip. The goalkeeper let Rivaldo's harmless shot slip out of his hands, right in front of Ronaldo's feet. No matter how hard he tried to reach the ball, he couldn't save it. As a result, Brazil had the lead and wouldn't let go of it for the rest of the game. And Kahn had a bad case of the blues: for a long time after the final whistle, he just leaned against the posts, and no consolation could make it better. ⚽

30 // December

"SEE? I told you so." Or at least this is what Pelé seems to be saying to Ronaldo: "You will become world champion and top scorer." But this of course isn't true. Pelé contributed a lot to World Cup history: glorious goals, three World Cup titles, and the crime-thriller *The World Cup Murder,* in which Gregor Ragusic, the Serbian coach of the USA team, is shot by evil communists. But, unfortunately, the prophetic talent of the greatest Brazilian player wasn't much better than his literary skills. In 1994, Pelé projected that Colombia would win the title—it was eliminated in the qualifying round. He guessed that an African team would win before the end of the twentieth century—not a single African country made it to the semifinal. In 1996, he predicted that Croatia would become the most successful European team—they fell out in the quarterfinal—and that Brazil would be world champion in 1998. However, they lost 0–3 in the final game. And, finally, in 2002, along with Franz Beckenbauer, he pegged France and Argentina as favorites. Lucky for Brazil! ⚽

31 // December

Soccer with glamour, an unusual image in the days of modern defensive soccer—but if any team can do it, Brazil, with its soccer wizardry, can. After the 2–0 final victory over Germany, Captain Cafu, who was the first player to have played in three championship finals, held the trophy up to the skies of Yokohama, filled with the lights of the stadium, confetti, and celebratory cheers. But Brazil wasn't the only team to gain recognition for its fifth world title, marking as it did the "return of the title to its spiritual home" (*The Guardian*). No, the brave Germans also wowed the entire world for the first time—and with a defeat, of all things. It was a picture-perfect end, as the Italian *Stampa* wrote: "Germany, which never gives up, is a worthy vice world champion. When Brazil wins, everyone's happy."

Afterword //

It all began as a rather arduous experience that the rest of the world hardly took note of: in 1930 several haphazardly selected teams embarked on a weeklong ocean journey to Uruguay to attend the first-ever soccer World Cup. Over the years it would turn into a billion-dollar worldwide spectacle, the current focus being Germany in 2006, the eighteenth world championship.

Before a single ball rolls over the pitch, this massive global entertainment event already is moving hearts and channeling corporate funds. Twelve stadiums, seating 600,000 spectators, were newly built or thoroughly modernized, at a cost of $1.66 billion, more than ten times what it cost to host the nine-stadium World Cup in 1974, the last time the games were held in Germany. Additionally, there's the cost of refurbishing the playing fields following the 2005–2006 championship season so that the thirty-two teams will play amid uniform conditions when they embark on the sixty-four-match tournament, beginning in Munich on June 9, with the final in Berlin on July 9.

Soon after the initial games in 1930, the World Cup established itself as a showcase of national confidence and pride for participating countries. Since then it has become equally important to the economy and image of the host nation.

Germany's economics minister, Wolfgang Clement, predicts that the event will generate profits of close to $10 billion—mainly through the one million international visitors expected to travel to the country. Other sources predict in addition that the games will spur economic growth of 0.5 percent, an increase in consumer spending of $3 billion to $4 billion, and tens of thousands of new jobs.

In order to ensure that not only the rich European nations benefit—owing to their greater means of winning the bid in the first place—FIFA decided that in the future the host nations will be selected by rotation.

The first country chosen by this principle for 2010 was South Africa, which only narrowly lost the bid to host the 2006 championship. Thus, after eighty years, the World Cup finally will move into a geographic realm hitherto all but off-limits—a realm, incidentally, that still has been overlooked by the planners of the only other comparable event, even after 110 years: the Olympic Games. The World Cup in Africa is evidence that soccer has finally come full circle, becoming a truly global sport.

The Author //

Christian Eichler was born in Wanne-Eickel, Germany, in 1959. After college, he worked as a certified librarian in several government ministries in Bonn between 1984 and 1988. While doing this, he was also a freelance sports journalist, writing articles for numerous publications (*Frankfurter Allgemeine Zeitung, Süddeutsche Zeitung, Kicker, Sportillustrierte, Die Welt* and *Die Welt am Sonntag*). In 1989 Eichler joined the sports editorial team of the *Frankfurter Allgemeine Zeitung,* which has won the award of Editorial Team of the Year eleven times.

In 1991 he was awarded the Grand Prize from the Organization of German Sports Journalists, and in 1994 he won the Fair Play Award for sports journalism. He's the author of the *Lexikon der Fußballmythen* (2002) *(Encyclopedia of Soccer Myths)*. Eichler is married and has two sons who aspire to become professional soccer players.

Project Manager, English-language edition: Magali Veillon

Editor, English-language edition: Michael Driscoll

Editorial Assistant, English-language edition: Aiah Wieder

Designer, English-language edition: Shawn Dahl

Production Manager, English-language edition: Colin Hough Trapp

Library of Congress Cataloging-in-Publication Data

Eichler, Christian, 1959-
  Soccer : 365 days / by Christian Eichler.
    p. cm.
  ISBN 13: 978-0-8109-5919-4 (hardcover) / ISBN 10: 0-8109-5919-4
  1. Soccer—History. 2. World Cup (Soccer)—History. I. Title.
  GV942.5.E53 2006
  796.33409—dc22
                          2005030390

Printed and bound in China
10 9 8 7 6 5 4 3 2

HNA ∎∎∎∎∎
harry n. abrams, inc.
a subsidiary of La Martinière Groupe
115 West 18th Street
New York, NY 10011
www.hnabooks.com

Knesebeck GmbH & Co. Verlags KG and Harry N. Abrams, Inc., are subsidiaries of LA MARTINIÈRE
GROUPE

Photograph Credits

© EMPICS: Jan 3–4, Jan 7, Jan 8 left, Jan 9, Jan 12 left,
Jan 16 left, Jan 21 right, Jan 22 right, Jan 23 right,
Jan 24, Feb 1 right, Feb 6 right, Feb 7, Feb 8 right,
Feb 13, Feb 15 left, Feb 20, Feb 22 right, Feb 23 right,
Feb 26 right, Mar 7 right, Mar 17 right, Mar 20 left,
Mar 21 right, Mar 26 right, Mar 27 right

Picture-Alliance/dpa: Jan 5–6, Jan 8 right, Jan 10–11,
Jan 12 right, Jan 13, Jan 14 right, Jan 15 right,
Jan 16 right, Jan 17, Jan 18 left, Jan 19 left, Jan 25 right,
Jan 26, Jan 27 right, Jan 28 right, Jan 29–31, Feb 2–4,
Feb 5 right, Feb 6 left, Feb 8 left, Feb 9 left, Feb 12,
Feb 15 right, Feb 16–19, Feb 21, Feb 23 left, Feb 24–25,
Feb 26 left

Picture–Alliance/ASA: Jan 15 left

AP/Wide World Photos: Page 3

imago sportfotodienst gmbh, Berlin: Pages 1, 2, 5–9,
Jan 1, Jan 14, Jan 18 right, Jan 19 right, Jan 23 left, Jan
27 left, Jan 28 left, Feb 5 left, Feb 9 right, Feb 11, Feb
14, Feb 22 left, Feb 28–Mar 6, Mar 7 left, Mar 8–Mar
16, Mar 18–19, Mar 20 right, Mar 22–25, Mar 26 left,
Mar 27 left, Mar 28–Dec 31, pages 740 and 742